FROM WITCHDOCTOR TO APOSTLE

THE STORY OF PAUL AI

May God bless you

Paul + Ruth

DR. PAUL AI

Published by:

VISION OUTREACH INTERNATIONAL
1705 Todds Lane,
Hampton, VA. 23666 - USA
Tel: 757.826.1426
Fax: 757.826.5436
Website: www.paulai.net
E-mail: dr.paulai@gmail.com

All Scripture quotations are taken from New International Version [NIV]and King James Version [KJV] of the Bible.

Design & Layout by Curry Advertising

ISBN: 978-967-10054-0-8

CONTENTS

PREFACE

Dr. Paul Ai's autobiography *"From Witchdoctor to Apostle"* is like the continuation of the Acts of the Apostles of the Bible. It is an amazing account of the power and grace of God in Dr. Paul Ai's life as well as the sacrifices of missionaries like Dr. John Hurston, Pastor Irvin Rutherford and the tremendous impact of mission-minded churches from the United States, Philippines, Korea and other parts of the world.

Thisbook is filled with real, dramatic stories of God's power that will bring tremendous encouragement to believers in challenging situations. Paul set his plough to the field and never looked back, resulting in the planting of hundreds and thousands of churches. In speed and urgency, he laborswith a deep conviction that the night comes when no man can work.

Paul shares Biblical Revelational Truths that were tested in the toughest situations in his life, including insights on how he planted churches in tough environments. It is a testimony of God's grace and power in the lives of those available for His service. His life and ministry areproof that the principle of giving not only appliesto rich nations. Paul experienced the blessing of giving and tithing even in prison – He became the richest prisoner! This should challenge the thinking of Christians from poorer nations who think that giving is only for the rich!

Rev. Dr. Joshua Yee
Lead Pastor
Renewal Lutheran Church, Malaysia

RECOMMENDATIONS

I have known Paul Ai before he and Ruth were married. He has always shown a servant's heart for fulfilling the Great Commission and has never deviated. Both of them have been willing to pay the price to see God's Kingdom established in the hearts of people, especially the Vietnamese people.

In "From Witchdoctor to Apostle", Paul tells us the story of God's grace in leading an individual and his family in total obedience to the will of God. New Testament faith is shown in this story of a life daily looking to the Father for provision and protection. Culturally it exposes the life of one, like the Apostle Paul in scripture, the adventure of someone who lived a life so foreign to most of us.

This is a great read and a wonderful modern day example of missionary service that reaches into many countries. It challenges our faith anew in this modern world of using great funding and great technology, when all that is required is simple faith. With little to help them, the Ai family has made an impact far beyond their limited resources and has shown us the power of the Gospel all over again through simple obedience and trust!

Irvin and Linda Rutherford
Founder and Executive Director
Global Ministry Teams

I was introduced to Paul via a telephone call by career missionary Irvin Rutherford, the president of Global Ministry Teams. Little did I know the impact that one phone call would have on my life and ministry! That has been over ten years ago, and since then I have had the privilege to work closely with this wonderful leader and to see firsthand the fruit of his life in Vietnam and across Southeast-Asia.

I know you will be thrilled and amazed as you read the real life account of a modern day apostle who like the apostles of old faced the wrath of the enemies of the gospel and proved again and again the faithfulness of the our Lord.

Rev. Ron Johnson
Lead Pastor – Markham Woods A/G
President – Foundations International

Paul Ai's "From Witchdoctor to Apostle" is a record of God's faithfulness. It also testifies that our God is a powerful God for "greater is He that is in us than he that is in the world". Read the book and your faith in Jesus will be reignited again to white-hot level! Truly, our God protects, empowers, provides and embraces us with His love. He is faithful to the very end."

Ps. Dr. Chew Weng Chee
Senior Pastor, SIBKL

I have known Pastors Paul and Ruth Ai for ten years since they first arrived in the United States. Pastor Paul is an apostle to the Vietnamese who does not quit. When he was put in the reeducation camps after the Communists overran South Vietnam in the 1970's, he could have quit but instead ministered to prisoners and prison guards alike. When he was released from prison only to face severe economic hardship in the 1980's, he could have quit but instead he received and imparted God's principles on prosperity to his disciples with fruit that remains.

When he was deported from his beloved Vietnam in the late 90's, he could have quit the ministry to live a comfortable life in the U.S. Instead he founded Vietnamese Outreach International and made disciples of Vietnamese living outside of Vietnam. If you like to read about thepower of God working through a modern day apostolic couple who does not quit in the face of multiple adversities, then this book is for you.

Steve Burke
Board Member, VOI

What an exciting and thrilling adventure into the heart of a true 21st century apostle of Jesus Christ! This book will challenge your faith and build it all at the same time!

Rev. Bruce A. Sonnenberg
Executive Director/ Founder
He Intends Victory, Irvine, California

Knowing Paul over the past ten years, I have witnessed firsthand the miracles of his ministry. Wherever he travels there is Apostolic ministry that takes place – souls are saved, churches are planted and disciples of Jesus Christ are made. Signs, wonders, and miracles signify his ministry. Paul has such a heart for people and is willing to put his life on the line for Jesus Christ. He is a devout follower of Jesus Christ, a dedicated husband and a loving father. Paul is a man of immense integrity and once he converted from witchdoctor to soul-winner for Jesus Christ, his passion for the things of the Lord has never diminished.

Prescott Belt
Lead Pastor
CELLebration Christian Fellowship

"Paul Aiand his wife Ruth are truly modern day apostles. God has done great works throughthis man of God's life, family and ministry. God's testimonies in Paul are more than inspirational and encouraging – they are transformational! One can't help but be amazed! My faith and vision for true discipleship has been so deeply challenged,and I believe yours will be also.

Rev. Dale Crall
College Pastor

The three words that best describe Paul and Ruth Ai are integrity, faith, and obedience. As you read Paul's story, you will see how God turned what was meant for evil into a testament to His power and love. You will see what God can do with a life of obedience. You will be encouraged to stand strong in the midst of trouble, and you will get a glimpse of God's desire for everyone to come to repentance and into a personal relationship with Himself.

Susan Goss
VOI Board Member

As General Superintendent of the Assemblies of God in Vietnam, Brother Ai was a fearless Christian leader and Pastor with a clear and compelling vision of the Great Commission, determined to reach the lost at any cost. He also discipled church members and helped provide pastoral training for the growth of the church in Vietnam.

Dr. David Yonggi Cho
Senior Pastor – Yoido Full Gospel Church
Chairman – World Pentecostal Fellowship

Intriguing! Inspiring! It reminds me of the Acts of the Apostles - of how God chooses and uses for His Glory. A wonderful autobiography that will build your faith!

Ps. Lawrence Yap.
Senior Pastor – CCC KL

DEDICATION

I have been saved and in the ministry for 40 years, and many people have invested into my life. I want to dedicate this book to the following people:

To God the Father for His love, God the Son for His salvation, and God the Holy Spirit for His power to do the work of the ministry for the past 40 years.

To my mom who really loved me and made sacrifices for me, encouraged me, and taught me. Even as a little boy, she taught me many things that have helped me in ministry today.

To Reverend Dr. John Hurston who led me out of darkness into light, out of the kingdom of Satan into the kingdom of God; and to his wife Maxine and his daughter Karen for their blessing and encouragement in my life.

To my wife, Ruth, who was willing to marry a "crazy preacher" and to leave a comfortable life in the big city of Saigon, to join me in winning souls and planting churches in the countryside and rural villages. Through suffering and poverty she always took care of me and encouraged me.

Even when she was alone while I was in prison, forced labor camp, and re-education camp, she cared for our children and planted two churches. I really appreciate this wonderful lady. She is a partner in my life with whom God blessed me.

To our four daughters, Baby Ruth, Mary, Esther, Elizabeth, and our son David, who really love the Lord Jesus, love missions, and pray and intercede for my wife and me as we travel to minister. They have been faithful to take care of things at home while we are away. They lead as a great example to other Christians and other pastors' children, and they are now partners with us in VOI and in our ministry. My wife and I are grateful to the Lord for our five children.

To Sister Susan and her husband Brother Matt Goss who really sacrificed their time to sit down with us to hear our story, and who went to Vietnam to see the reality of life and to meet the people. This couple spent a lot of their hours, days, weeks, months, and even years to assist us since we arrived in the United States in 1999.

Even after ten years, they are still with us and have helped us write this book. Without this couple, this book would never have been written. Even though many people have tried, it never happened until this couple sacrificed their time to help us.

I really appreciate all of these people for their sacrifice, their warmth and fellowship, and contributions to my life and my ministry.

It is my desire that this book will glorify God and encourage many people to follow Jesus and to join us in bringing people out of darkness into light, out of the kingdom of Satan into the kingdom of God. Together, we will enlarge His kingdom and bring Him glory!

ACKNOWLEDGEMENTS

Paper, ink, and space in this little book will not allow me to recognize and thank all of the people who have made sacrifices and investments into my life, and have blessed my ministry in so many ways, but here are some of them:

Pastor Ron Johnson, former senior pastor of Bethel Temple in Hampton, Virginia, thank you very much for your trust in me to first bring me out of "Hanoi Hilton" and then to bring me and my family out of Vietnam into Hampton, Virginia. You are the one who opened the door for me to worldwide ministry. Thank you.

Reverend Irvin Rutherford, you have been a great friend since 1974; even though your hair color and your size have changed, your warm heart is still the same! You are really a true apostle and a true friend. You have connected me and Ruth with many different people and many different networks to enlarge God's kingdom. Thank you, Brother Irvin.

Reverend Dr. David Yonggi Cho, thank you for your encouragement to Ruth and me. Thank you for your love and care for us. You have really blessed us, particularly while I was in prison. You not only sent emails, cards and made phone calls, but your office sent out news to people around the world so they would know how to pray for us.

And whenever I am in Korea, you always bless me with a great blessing. Thank you very much, Dr. Cho.

Board of Directors of Vietnamese Outreach International: Dr. Karen Hurston, Reverend John Anderegg, Reverend Ron Johnson, Reverend Bruce Sonnenberg, Reverend Prescot Belt, Reverend Wayne Murray, Reverend Glenn Reynolds, Sister Susan Goss, Brother Steve Burke, and Reverend Ruth Kim, thank you very much for giving me your time, you knowledge, your experience, even your finances, and your network of connections for VOI. Thank you very much.

Pastors, churches, and individuals, who are VOI Partners, thank you very much for partnering with Ruth and me and with Vietnamese Outreach International. Many of you have sent us to Laos, Cambodia, Malaysia, Korea, and even Kuwait to enlarge the kingdom of God. Thank you.

Reverend Joshua Yee, Dr. Carey Yee, and the Renewal Lutheran Church in Malaysia, thank you for your wonderful partnership with us as we reach out to Vietnamese in that area and in Cambodia.

Vietnam Veterans, thank you very much. You went to Vietnam years ago with M16 rifles, but you became forerunners for missionaries. Because of you, doors were opened for missionaries to come to Vietnam with "John 3:16 Bibles." Thank you.

Assembly of God of USA, the A/G of Philippines, A/G of Korea, and World Assembly of God Fellowship, thank you for your encouragement to us.

Reverend Henry Swain, thank you for your inspiring teaching in our Bible college in Vietnam.

Reverend Carrie Hunsberger, thank you very much for your anointed teaching and impartation into our lives.

Reverend Wes Hurst and Reverend Lester Keeney, thank you for your wonderful leadership and encouragement to us in the early years of the Assembly of God in Vietnam.

Reverend Nam Soo Kim from Korea, Reverend Celso Sumida, Reverend Joey Tupe, Reverend Luciano Cariaga, and Reverend Pedro Belardo from the Philippines, thank you for your wonderful teachings and exemplary living. You walked the way you talked, and you left a wonderful example for me. It would have been very difficult for me to overcome all the difficulties and persecution in Vietnam if you had not equipped me and had lived your lives as my role models. Thank you for investing into my life.

People who partner with Open Doors, Christ to Thailand Mission, Christ to the Phillipines Mission, and with Tribes in Nations Outreach, thank you for your encouragement. When I was in prison you visited my family and encouraged my wife and my children. You blessed us.

Brother Max Moody in Tallahassee, Florida, thank you for your heart toward us and toward the ministry since we first met years ago in Vietnam, even until now.

Sister Lorrie Croxton, Sister Jonell McFadden, and other friends, thank you for your time invested in joining Sister Susan to help correct and complete this book.

Brother Matthew Philippose and family in Malaysia, thank you for your wonderful friendship and your help to us since we met six years ago.

Brothers and sisters in Vietnamese Harvest Network International in Laos, Cambodia, Vietnam, and United States, thank you for your cooperation and encouragement to us.

Again, thank you to everyone who has invested into our lives and ministry. Through me and my wife, we are together imparting and investing into many other lives for God's glory and for His kingdom's sake.

May the Lord bless you, and together we will advance His kingdom while we are here on earth to prepare for the day that we will rejoice together with the fruit of our labor in Heaven!

PROLOGUE

"Paul, I have some great news for you," Ruth, my wife, said as we were crossing the border from Cambodia into Vietnam. We were traveling home from an extended visit in Cambodia.

This was a pleasant interruption from the thoughts that I was having about the Christian leaders we had recently trained in Cambodia. I was praying that the pastors who attended the training would make it safely back to their homes in Vietnam. It was likely that they would be questioned at the border regarding the purpose for their visit into Cambodia. If the security police learned that they had been to Cambodia for Christian training, they would likely be arrested and put into prison.

Now I turned my attention to my wife. God had blessed me so wonderfully with a strong and godly wife. We had been married for eleven years, and had four daughters. "What is it?" I asked her. "Honey, you won't believe this," she said, "but I'm pregnant again!" "That's wonderful!" I replied.

My mind quickly raced back twenty years when a curse was placed on me – that I would never have a male child. In Vietnam, if you do not have a son, you do not have a future.

Since there is no insurance or retirement fund, the male child is the one who cares for the parents as they get older. Before I became a Christian, I was a witchdoctor, and the curse was in retaliation for leaving the group.

When my wife announced she was pregnant, I knew in my spirit that this would be our son. I told her, "Honey, the curse is broken. Our son is on the way!" I was not sure she believed me. After four girls, would we really be having a son?

A few hours later when we arrived at our home in Saigon, we were greeted by 37 police officers eagerly waiting to take me to prison. This was not anything new for me, as I had been arrested numerous times, and had been in and out of prison and forced labor camps over the past fifteen years.

As usual, I was accused of illegal activities of preaching the Bible, starting churches, and training Christians.

This time I was sentenced without receiving a trial to nine years in prison, forced labor camp, and re-education camp.

KINGDOM OF DARKNESS | 1

In 1970, twenty-one years before my arrest in Saigon, I certainly had no understanding what lay ahead for my life. I was nineteen years old and was one of the top witchdoctors in my region.

I was raised in a Buddhist home, and at age nine I was sent to the local pagoda to train as a Buddhist monk. Young boys were sent to pagodas for various reasons. Sometimes, it was a sign of wealth, other times, it was a commitment that the mother made before the child was born, or if a boy was an orphan he would be raised by the monks.

My grandfather and parents sent me to pagoda so that I could learn to live a disciplined life. I was a very energetic, mischievous, and courageous boy. I already was supervising people who worked on my grandfather's farm, although I lacked the discipline and maturity that was required for that role.

By going to the pagoda, I would learn the wise and disciplined ways of Buddhist monks. My family wanted me to build moral character and earn good "spiritual credit" so that I would be better in the next life. My grandfather was a very wealthy Chinese medical doctor, and my father was the town mayor.

When I was born they named me Tran Dinh Ai which means, "stop loving the world." They believed that by training to be a monk, I could avoid the corruption of politics and the lure of wealth.

In the pagoda I was required to learn three baskets full of books that contained Buddhist teachings, clean the idols of Buddha, and recite various prayers that were assigned. When we were mischievous and got into trouble, our punishment was to go to the prayer tower where we had to recite prayers all day long.

The Pagoda was not my only schooling. I still had to learn math, science, history, reading and writing. Since my grandfather and parents were very wealthy, they paid for a tutor to come to the house or to the pagoda to teach me.By the time I was fifteen years old, I had reached a high level in Buddhism. The level I reached was similar to being an ordained minister in Christianity.

In Buddhism, this accomplishment was based on the number of people who came to me for prayer and who were my followers. I was now a practicing monk. As a monk, I thought that I would really be able to help people with their problems.

What I realized, however, was that becoming a monk was more about being selfish. It seemed more

focused on how to be better than someone else, rather than having the ability to help other people.

In my search for power, I began to attend witchcraft meetings. I saw that these witchdoctors had power to do things that they could not humanly do. For example, I saw them cut themselves in different places on their bodies without any

Day of Witch Master Ordination

bleeding. I was intrigued and desired to have the same ability to do supernatural things. It was certainly more interesting to me that being a Buddhist monk, and with power like that, I certainly could help a lot of people.

So at fifteen, I began to study and practice witchcraft. After only two years, I became so good that I advanced to witch master, the next level above witchdoctor. This meant that I had other witchdoctors as my disciples.

I pledged myself to hundreds of categories of gods, each group with a different power that I wanted or thought that I needed. In order to receive the power of a certain god, I had to study what ritual would attract the god, perform the ritual and incantation, and then add the tattoo to my body. The tattoo was a sign that I had the power of that group of gods. Two of the categories of gods that I selected were wood gods and metal gods. By having these gods, I would be protected from anything or anyone that tried to harm me by using anything made of wood or metal.

Tattoos representing 3366 gods

I was serving a total of 3,366 gods, and under those gods I was able to perform miracles with signs and wonders. For example, in my neighborhood, one of my father's distant relatives was very rich from being corrupt. He thought that he did not need any gods because he was rich.

I prayed for a group of gambling gods to attack him. For three nights in a row he went out gambling and lost all the money that he had. His wife even tried to hide some of it so the collectors would not take all of it, but the gods led them to where the money was hidden.

Another time, the police came to my house to search for me. They searched the entire house but the gods blinded their eyes and they could not find me. The entire time they were there, I was in the same room with them, watching everything that they were doing.

Many people came to me because they needed a great miracle. In the spirit world the miracles that you expect depend on your faith, and your faith is demonstrated by the offering that you bring. People expected great miracles so they brought big offerings, and as a result, I became very wealthy. I prayed for people to be healed and they were healed. I prayed blessings over their homes, and they would experience an increase in crops or finances.

I began to realize the more those gods gave me power, the more they bound my life under their strongholds. The power of Satan only brings people from life to death. My desire to help people was still there, but it became more difficult to control the power I possessed because the gods were actually controlling me. At times, instead of helping people, I cursed them as a form of revenge, or as a way to teach them a lesson. I became a slave to the kingdom of darkness.

During the time that I was coming under the power of darkness in Vietnam, Dr. John Hurston was helping a young Dr. Yonggi Cho grow the world's largest church in Korea. In 1970, Cho sent Hurston and a team of Filipino, Korean, and American missionaries to Vietnam to preach the Gospel. They came to my town in central Vietnam (Quang Nam Da Nang) to preach the Gospel.

At first, I ignored them.Many religions and even Christian denominations had come to Vietnam to hold crusades. Nothing of significance ever happened. These groups usually left the witchdoctors alone because they were afraid of us, and we had no real interest in them because they had little effect on our operations.

Typically, we were able to use our magic to hinder their efforts. To me, this group was no different, so I did not give much attention to them the first three nights. After three nights, however, my whole town was shaken.

My witchcraft students came to me and said, "Master, you need to come and shut down this Christian meeting." I said, "What's going on?" They replied, "Sir, since those missionaries have come to our town and preached their religion, many of our customers have left us!"

"They have joined with them, and that number keeps increasing every night! You must come and stop them; otherwise, we will lose all of our customers and we will lose our town!"

The witchcraft doctors and fortunetellers were angry when they saw what was happening. They were angry because this meant that they were losing clients. I was angry too, so I went to the Christian meeting. I had been trained in religious activity, so I expected to see the missionaries just move their hands, and conduct religious rituals and ceremonies like witchcraft and voodoo.

When I went to the crusade, I was disappointed to find them singing what they called "worship" or "praise" to the Lord. It was strange to me because they were not only singing, but they clapped their hands too. Some of them were even dancing and jumping up and down.

The way they worshipped was noisy to the Vietnamese people. This was not a religion to me because religions were to keep quiet, worship, and meditate; this was different. I was disappointed.

After all of the noisy worship, they opened the Bible and read the story of Jesus Christ. They explained, "When Jesus was on the earth, the people who followed Him were noisy because they witnessed the signs and wonders He performed."

"Jesus came to heal people, solve their problems, and to change their lives. He made the blind see, the dumb talk, and the lame walk.Jesus came to help people and to solve their daily life problems."

The missionaries stated that they did not come to bring the Vietnamese people another religion because, "All religion does is make people religious. Jesus didn't come to bring you religion, because all religions with their religious activity will weigh you down.Jesus Christ said, 'Come unto me all who labor and are heavy burdened, and I will give you rest.'"

"Jesus did not come to give you more loads of care because He knows that people have more than enough troubles to handle. He came to give people rest. So, instead of bringing you religion, we bring you Jesus. If you have troubles in your life, just come. Jesus will lift your load."

During the war in Vietnam, people had all kinds of troubles, so many Vietnamese accepted Jesus as their Lord and Savior. They gave their burdens to Him. The missionaries prayed for them and then everyone got noisy again. After that, they opened the Bible and said, "Jesus Christ is the same yesterday, today, and forever. He healed people. He delivered people. He comforted people. He is here today! If you have any need, just come to Jesus."

They opened the Bible and read *Acts26:16-18.*

> *"'Now get up and stand on your feet. I have appeared to you to appoint you as a servant and as a witness of what you have seen of me and what I will show you. I will rescue you from your own people and from the Gentiles. I am sending you to them to open their eyes and turn them from darkness to light, and from the power of Satan to God, so that they may receive forgiveness of sins and a place among those who are sanctified by faith in me.'"*

They continued, "Friends, we want to assure you that we are not going to bring you a new religion, but we want to bring you Jesus. Jesus came not to start an establishment of religion, but He came to bring you out of darkness into light, out of Satan unto God."

"Jesus Christ came to set you free, to deliver you. If you come with any burden, any problem, Jesus Christ is greater than all of your problems. He is greater than all of your burdens. Come, and Jesus will meet all of your needs."

Many Vietnamese came forward. This line was longer than the one I saw earlier. The missionaries began to pray for them, and they were noisier than the first time!

After they prayed, they made an announcement, "Who among you in the past few nights that have been here and were prayed for, and God answered our prayer? Would you please come forward and share your testimony about what God did for you?"

I am telling you, this line was even longer than the first two! People began to share their testimonies of how God had healed their sicknesses, set them free, and delivered them from smoking, drinking and other addictions.

As I heard each person speak, I began to think that the foreign missionaries had hired my own people to advertise for their religion. If they continued to push this religion, sooner or later I was going to lose my customers and control of my town. I had to do something to stop it.

So, that first night, I called upon 1,000 gods. By the end of the service, I realized that none of the gods I called upon had shown up to stop the crusade. I left frustrated that night. I went home and decided to fast the following day and spend time calling upon the 3,366 gods that I served.

I went back the next evening and the same thing was going on – worship, noisy singing, preaching, praying and people turning to Jesus. I called on 2,000 gods this time, but again, by the end of the service I realized that none of my gods showed up to shut down the crusade for me.

I left more frustrated than the night before. I went home and decided that I would not sleep. I had to stay awake to arouse my 3,366 gods.They needed to come back with me the next evening to shut down the Christian meeting before I lost my town.

The next evening, I arrived early and parked my 50cc moped in the parking lot. Since there were a lot of thieves during the war in Vietnam, I prayed and commanded 20 gods, "Do nothing, but stay in this parking lot and take care of my moped, so no one will take it away from me."

On the way into the church, I stopped by the generator.

I prayed, laid hands on it, and commanded another 20 gods, "Do nothing, but stay here and mess up the generator, so they have no electricity for their crusade tonight." Next, I walked into the meeting area and went over to their equipment, lights, and sound system.

Visiting the Christian Crusade Meeting
(In dark shirt, standing in front)

I prayed and commanded another 20 gods, "Mess up their equipment, so they are not able to worship their God tonight." In the kingdom of darkness that I served while doing witchcraft, I learned that the devil hates to see Christians worship their God.After becoming a Christian, I read the Bible and learned:*"But thou art holy, O thou that inhabitest thepraises of Israel."*Psalm 22:3 (KJV)

God is present in the worship of His people. When God is present, liberation, deliverance, and salvation will take place. People will be set free and the devil will lose more and more followers as they turn to and believe in God. That is why the devil does not want to see Christians worship a living God.

After I commanded 20 gods to ruin the equipment, I kept calling on the 3,366 gods that I had faithfully served for many years. Tonight, after subtracting the 20 gods left to guard my moped, the 20 gods to mess up the generator, and 20 gods to mess up the sound and lighting systems, there were 3,306 gods left that were called to show up and shut down this missionary crusade.

During the service, I went to a corner and prayed to group after group of my gods. I called name after name for more than two hours.The Christian activities still continued. People came to accept Jesus. People came to ask for prayers for healing, for deliverance, and for solving problems.People came to share their testimonies.

Even some of my followers that were praying against the crusade with me that night joined the Christians! As it continued, the number of people that left me increased. I was angry and began to call upon my gods harder and louder. By the end of the service, in the spirit, I recognized that none of the 3,366 gods showed up to do the job they were supposed to do when I commanded them.

I was confused and struggling with what I should do next. I needed to stop this Christian activity. Then I heard an announcement, "If anyone of you has any question that hinders or prevents you from coming to accept Jesus; even though, you have seen signs, wonders, and miracles, we would love to sit down with you and help you find the answers for the questions you have." I thought, "Oh, this is a great opportunity for me."

I went up front. I told them who I was, what I did, and why I was there. I saw all the things that had happened that night and that all of my people had left me. "I wonder if you can answer all of my questions. I was thinking about joining you too, but if you cannot answer all of my questions, then you had better pack up, leave my town, and leave all of my people alone."

The missionaries said, "Sir, we do not know if we can satisfy you by answering all of your questions, but we will have our God, through His Word, the Bible, to help you find the answers."

I thought I had the upper hand in this deal since I was trained as a Buddhist monk and now I was a witch master. I was going to raise the tough questions so that they would not be able to answer them. I thought, "Once I have proven they cannot answer the questions, the missionaries will have to pack up and leave my town."

Hour after hour, all of my tough questions were answered through the book they called the Holy Bible. Through this book, the book of truth, they led me to a place where I realized that He – The Living God, is greater than the 3,366 gods I worshiped *(1 John 4:4b – "...because the One Who is in you is greater than the one who is in the world.")*. Of course, I lost the battle. I am glad I lost though, because now I have won in Jesus' name!

Standing up from the pulpit, I was so excited. I ran back to the parking lot, eager to drive home to tell the story. When I got to the parking lot, I could not find my moped. I walked around for ten minutes looking for it. Now, I really understood why my 3,366 gods did not show up to shut down the Christian crusade – they had all disappeared with my moped!

Here, I realized something else, even the devil can perform some signs, wonders, and miracles. Through the Word of God though, I found out that all the devil's miracles only take people in one direction: from life to death.

The reason Jesus performed signs, wonders, and miracles was to bring people from death to life.

"The thief comes only to steal and kill and destroy; I have come that they may have life, and have it to the full."
John 10:10

I had to walk over an hour to get home that night. Along the way, the devil attacked my mind. He tried to bring me back to his kingdom of darkness, but I had made up my mind to follow Jesus.

I was shocked when I walked in my house. It was late and my grandparents, my parents, and my relatives were waiting for me. My grandfather looked at me and said, "Oh, grandson, I'm glad that you are home, but you know what, the news has already spread throughout the whole town. Everybody wondered what you were doing tonight, grandson. Were you trying to mock the missionaries? Or are you serious about Jesus?"

I said, "Grandpa, I am serious about Jesus Christ." My grandfather was angry, "What happened to you? Grandson, you were sent to a Buddhist temple to train as a Buddhist monk. You quit. You wanted to study witchcraft. Yes, we sent you to witchcraft training."

"After years and years of training, you have become a witchcraft master with 3,366 gods. Are you not satisfied? You quit again? What is wrong with you? What is wrong with Buddha?" I looked at my grandfather, and said, "Sir, Grandpa, there is nothing wrong with Buddha."

"I respect Buddha highly, but I do have one problem." He said, "What's the problem?" I said, "The more I studied Buddhism, the more disappointed I became. I saw that Buddha and his teachings were good, and he tried to live a good life. He was a very wealthy prince, and he left all his wealth and status to search for the meaning of life.

As he observed people in his travels, he began to realize that life was meaningless. He searched for truth and for hope, but he only found despair. In his travels and through his experiences, he thought of some very wise teachings, but he never found the truth until after he died.

"Grandfather, I realized that Buddhism looks good, but that it is really negative. It looks positive, but really there is no hope. To me, it is like sinking in the ocean and there is no one and nothing to keep you from sinking."

"You know, in Buddhism, we believe that if we do everything that is good we can earn credit toward nirvana, the end to suffering caused by desire. If we do not desire, then we do not suffer."

"In reality, however, we cannot live a good life; we cannot earn this credit by being good because we are born with a natural bent to sin and cannot stop sinning, no matter how hard we try."

"Grandfather, we all know deep in our hearts that this is true. What happens is that we only feel hopelessness in Buddhism because we know that what they are doing is not really helping us attain that for which we are seeking. It is like a feeling of sinking in the ocean with no one to help."

"The more I studied about Buddha and the Buddhist doctrine, the more I realized that I could not find power to keep me from sinking. Buddha had a wonderful teaching and was wise, but the problem is, even though Buddha was a good guy and a nice guy, he died, and he is still dead."

"That is why I became a witchdoctor. As a witchdoctor, at least I had power. When I went to the Christian meeting, however, none of my powers worked. Nothing I did could stop them from singing and praying to their God, and nothing stopped their God from healing them."

"When I talked with the missionaries, they answered my questions from their Book, the Bible. I asked them where their God was and how He was real. They described how He is different than Buddha or witchcraft."

As I gave my long explanation, my grandfather became angrier and interrupted me, "What about Christ?" I quickly summarized, "Sir, Christ is not only a guy, not only wise, not only nice, not only died, but He arose from the dead. He is alive and He is in control!"

My grandfather was so angry, "Shut your mouth, grandson! For years, I have invested into your life and now after one night, you have changed your mind and you try to preach to me. Listen, you need to go to bed, rest well, and think carefully. Tomorrow morning, before breakfast, you need to inform me whether you tried to mock these missionaries or not. If you did, then everything will be all right. Otherwise, you will have to leave this family without any inheritance. We will disown you."

This was difficult. A little over an hour ago, I gave my heart to Jesus and lost my moped. Now, I am about to lose everything. I went to bed but was not able to go to sleep. I kept turning back and forth, and I wondered what I was going to do.

Of course, I did not want to pray to my own gods again, but I did not know how to pray to Jesus because this was new to me. From deep within my heart, I cried out, "Jesus, I don't know how to pray to You, but I do need You. Help me. What should I do?"

I am glad that as I cried from my heart to Jesus that He heard my cry. The power of the Holy Spirit showed up in my room in an incredible way. Forty years ago, the missionaries did not have PowerPoint or an overhead projector, so new songs had to be memorized. Songs were taught sentence by sentence, verse by verse to make sure everyone could sing and memorize.

As a witchdoctor, I never opened my mouth to sing any of their songs, but I did not plug my ears. As the songs entered my ears; they sank into my heart. At the moment I needed God the most, I cried out from the bottom of my heart and God showed up.

He brought one of the songs to my mind and I began to sing. *"I have decided to follow Jesus. I have decided to follow Jesus. No turning back. No turning back. The cross before me; the world behind me. No turning back. No turning back."* I do not remember how many times I sang that song, but I sang until I went to sleep. I slept like a baby.

My grandfather woke me up the next morning. He yelled, "Grandson, what is your decision?" I was still groggy after a night of spiritual battle, so he yelled louder, "What is your decision?" Now I was awake, and scared. He shouted louder and louder and I could not think of what to say.

My grandfather was an old Chinese medical doctor who did not take kindly to disagreement. My dad had trained me not to answer too quickly when he was upset. "You have to draw a long wide circle around him and try to calm him down before you respond to him. Otherwise, you will be in a lot of trouble."

His face was red, so I knew he was mad. I was terrified. I did not know how to delay answering his question so that I could calm him down. He yelled louder. I opened my mouth, but instead of responding with a question, I sang this song, *"I have decided to follow Jesus; no turning back; no turning back."* That song made him very angry.

He said, "Grandson, it is time for you to leave this family without any inheritance, and don't turn back to this home unless you refuse your Jesus."

It was very difficult for me. I wondered what I was going to do and where I was going to stay. Then another song came to me. It was:

> *"Many things about tomorrow*
> *I don't seem to understand.*
> *But I know who holds tomorrow and*
> *I know He holds my hand."*

THE CURSE | 4

My family was in an uproar because of my choice. As I was singing, "I have decided to follow Jesus," there was a knock at the door. I opened the door and there stood one of the witchdoctors. My grandfather yelled, "What are you doing here?" The witchdoctor replied, "Sir, doctor, there's a rumor around town that brother Ai has quit worshiping our gods and he has joined with the Christians. So, my master sent me here to try to bring brother Ai back to witchcraft." Grandfather said, "Good. Try to bring him back; bring him back!"

This witchcraft doctor walked in and asked, "Brother Ai is this rumor true?" I said, "Yes, it is true." He asked, "What's wrong? What happened to you? You were trained to be a Buddhist monk. You were not satisfied with Buddha. You came to study witchcraft and you became a witchcraft master and now you have quit again. Friend, let's sit down and talk."

So we sat down and talked. We discussed, debated, and argued heavily. Finally, I came to a place where I was able to say, "Friend, you know, even though I served 3,366 gods, deep in my heart, I was lonely, empty and worried. I didn't know what was going to happen to us in the future. But now I have found that Jesus has a bright future for us and He has a bright future for me."

He looked at me strangely and asked, "Brother Ai, what do you mean? As a witch doctor and a fortune teller, when people had problems they always came to you. You looked at their face, read their palms, and told them their future. So you mean to tell me, you don't know your future?"

I said, "Friend, that's what I want to discuss with you. When people were worried about their future, they came to the witchdoctors and fortune tellers. They expected us to tell them their future. After we told them their future, they were more worried than before." He asked, "Why?" I said, "Well, fortune tellers don't really know your future. The only thing they know about your future is that it gets darker, darker, and darker.

But the Word of God in Jeremiah 29:11 *says, 'God said, 'For I have a plan for you. My plan is not to harm you, but to bless you and prosper you.'* God desires a future for us, not one that will harm us, but one that blesses us and prospers us. God desires a bright future for us."

At the end of that story, this witchcraft doctor knelt down and accepted Jesus as his Lord and Savior. Now, witchcraftlost a second doctor! Within that first week, I led seven witchcraft doctors to the Lord, and they became my first cell group.

After losing these doctors to the Lord, the coven leaders decided they would not send anyone else to meet with me. Instead, they met together and prayed to send a curse on me. "Mr. Ai is never going to have a son, and therefore no future," they declared. It is a strong tradition in Vietnam to have a son. When you get old, your son is supposed to take care of you. He is in essence your 'future' so to speak and thus, they cursed me to erase my future.

Through reading the Bible, however, I discovered that Jesus came to save our souls and to bring us out of darkness into light, from Satan unto God. He also breaks the curses from many generations past, so I prayed and claimed deliverance from all the curses that had been spoken over me.

David, our son, at age 6

During the first ten years that my wife and I were married, there was no evidence that the curse had been broken. We had four girls: Ruth, Mary, Esther, and Elizabeth. Everyone said there was no way that we were going to have a son.

In 1991, on the way back to Vietnam from training pastors in Cambodia, my wife told me that she was pregnant again. I told her, "Our son is on the way!"Following my arrest when we arrived in Saigon, my wife was not allowed to see me. After two years she was given permission to visit me in prison. As she walked up she was holding hands with a little boy.

Our five children: Ruth, Mary, Esther, Elizabeth, David

When she came closer, I realized this was our son. The curse had been broken!Ruth said, "You know you always told people, 'Believe in the Lord Jesus Christ and you and your household will be saved.'" "You believe in deliverance. And here, God not only delivered you, but since our son was born, most of your relatives have accepted Jesus. Over 300 of your relatives have come to know Jesus as Lord and Savior!" I was very excited. They saw the evidence of the power of God and recognized Him as the one true God and Savior.

MY LIFE CHANGES | 5

I was disowned by my family and rejected by my community when I made my decision to follow Jesus in 1970. When I was asked to leave my family's house, the Filipino missionaries in the area graciously allowed me to move in with them. I lived with them for one year, during which I learned what it meant to live as a Christian and what it meant to minister to others.

We traveled on foot to many villages to preach the Gospel and win souls for Christ. Since the missionaries spoke English and were not yet fluent in Vietnamese, I was their interpreter. This is how I learned to preach. There was no opportunity to spend a lot of time studying theology in the beginning of my walk with the Lord.

I grew very quickly in my faith because I read the Bible and believed what I read. I was hungry for the Lord, and He filled that hunger with the Word and His Holy Spirit. I also had to declare freedom from the demonic gods that I had served. This meant that I had to renounce each group of gods, cancel the covenant I had made with them, and proclaim the new covenant I had in Jesus.

I never thought I would be a pastor, but when the witchdoctors accepted Jesus, they had a lot of questions. I was already conducting Bible studies with them to share what the Holy Spirit was teaching me.

We were growing in the Lord together. My friends and other people in town also began to ask questions about why I joined this Christian group. I shared the Gospel with them and prayed for healing and deliverance for them, and people began to be drawn to the Lord. We started holding services by the light of the full moon since we did not have electricity.

This made me realize that I needed theological training to be able to continue to disciple and lead people. So, I attended Bible school in 1971, first in Da Nang, then in Vung Tau.I had wonderful Bible teachers at the school such as Dr. John and Maxine Hurston, Reverend Henry

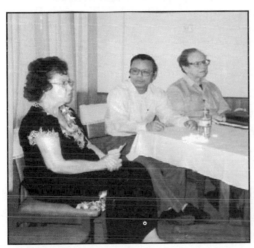

Dr.John Hurston (right) and his wife, Maxine (left), return to Vietnam after 20 years

Swain, Pastor Glenn Stafford and his wife, and also Pastor CarrieHunsburger, who was the first woman missionary teacher to Vietnam.

Some of the guest lecturers and speakers that visited the Bible school would go on to play key roles in my life, such as Reverend Aaron Rothganger, Reverend Wes Hurst, Pastor Lester Keeney, Pastor Wes Wesley, and Reverend Irvin Rutherford from the U.S.

There were also guest lecturers and speakers from Korea, France, and the Philippines including Pastor Nam Soo Kim, Pastor Amé Cizeron, Pastor Celso Sumida, Pastor Joey Tupe, Pastor Luciano Cariaga, and Pastor Pedro Belardo.

The connections that God was making continued with many Catholic priests and nuns who came from their seminaries to the Bible school to study about the Holy Spirit, and with many brothers and sisters from South Vietnam.

The highlight for me in Bible school was learning from the Catholic priests like Father Bach-Van-Loc, Father Le-Van-Thi, Father Dinh-Khac-Tieu, and many of the nuns. They were filled with the Holy Spirit, really on fire for the Lord, and helped me grow in my understanding of the Holy Spirit's work in my life.

I finished Bible school and began working full-time as a minister. Soon, I became part of the General Council of the Assemblies of God in Vietnam.

From 1970 to 1975, South Vietnam had not yet fallen to Communism, so we were still free to worship God openly.

The church was growing in Vung Tau where the Bible school was located; in the refugee camps of Tam-Phuoc and Long Thanh; in Phan-Rang and in Da-Lat; in Saigon where the headquarters of the Assemblies of God (A/G) were located; in my hometown of Quang Nam, Da Nang; and in the town of Tam-Ky.

Under the Republic of South Vietnam, which was supported by Americans, the Church had total freedom and was growing rapidly. Then, in 1975, when the last helicopter left the American embassy in Saigon, all missionaries were forced to leave the country.

TheA/G leadership came together to pray and seek the Lord for direction for what they needed to do next. After we prayed, we all agreed, "Let's get on the van, drive to the riverbank and find a boat. We will get on the boat and get out of Vietnam as quick as we can before the Communists take over and put us in jail."

I was so eager when I heard this announcement because I remembered a prophecy given to me a few years prior by Maxine Hurston.

She told me, "God has called you and has chosen you. He says, 'Even though you face trials and difficulties, be faithful to Me. If you will be faithful to Me, I will be faithful to you. I will raise you as a leader of the Church in the nation of Vietnam."

"If you are faithful to Me, then build My church in Vietnam. I will raise you up as a leader. I will make you to become the father of many. If you are faithful to Me, I will not only put you in the position of leadership, but I will actually send you out into the world as an apostle to prepare My Church for the rapture.'"

This was a wonderful prophecy, so as I prepared to get on the boat, I thought, "This is the time for me to travel around the world as an apostle." But then the Holy Spirit told me, "No." I was the General Secretary of the Assemblies of God in Vietnam, but I did not want to listen to the voice of the Holy Spirit right then. I did not want to stay in Vietnam and be put in jail by the Communists, so, I just kept quiet.

I got on the van with the other pastors and friends. We arrived at the boat and I proceeded to board with everyone else. When I was on board, ready to say good-bye to Vietnam, the Holy Spirit spoke to me again, "Paul Ai, what are you doing on this boat? Are you going to be a Jonah on this boat?"

When I heard this question, I got scared. My face turned blue, and I began to sweat. I thought, "Well, no, I don't want to be like Jonah. He ran away from what God instructed him to do and nearly caused everyone on the boat to lose their lives."

My friends looked at me. "Brother Ai, what has happened to you? Are you seasick?" they asked. I said, "No, I am not seasick, but I am shaken by what the Holy Spirit just spoke to me." They were thrilled. They asked, "Brother Ai, we are about to make a very dangerous journey on the ocean, and we need a word from the Lord. What has God spoken to you, brother?"

I replied, "The Holy Spirit asked me, 'What are you doing on this boat? Do you want to be a Jonah?'" They quickly replied, "Brother Ai, you had better get out of this boat! We don't want to take Jonah with us on this journey!" After I got off the boat, I felt sorry for myself. I thought, "I was so stupid! I should not have told them that. I should have just kept quiet. I could have left Vietnam with them and been an apostle around the world."

It was too late to change my mind, though, so I got back on the van and drove back to church. The song came back to me, "Many things about tomorrow I don't seem to understand. But I know who holds tomorrow and I know He holds my hand."

I watched the last of the American soldiers leave Saigon, and I thought back over what had transpired since they arrived in 1965. Many of us were grateful for what the Americans did. They had brought to South Vietnam a taste of peace, democracy and growth in our economy. After the many years of war Vietnam had experienced with various countries, people began to have hope.

In fact, because the U.S. government sent soldiers with M-16 rifles, the Church could send missionaries with "John 3:16 Bibles!" Through the Word and the power of the Holy Spirit, many Vietnamese came to know the Lord Jesus Christ as the Way, the Truth, and the Life.

I began to prepare for Sunday's sermon, wondering what I would preach the first Sunday under communism. As a Pentecostal minister, I had been trained to seek the Lord for the message that He has for His people, so I prayed and began to search from Genesis to Revelation, but nothing came to me.

I continued seeking the Lord for what to preach until Saturday night. Still, nothing came to me. When I woke up Sunday morning, I expected that I would receive a special message from the Lord for His people. Still, there was nothing.

I thought, "Okay, if I don't have any message from the Lord, I will just ask the men serving as elders and deacons to share their testimonies and their ideas. Then I will summarize all the testimonies and ideas as a sermon."

It was 8:00 in the morning and time for me to prepare the building for people's arrival. Pastors in Vietnam live in the parish house behind the church, and are responsible for everything: maintenance, security, cleaning, and unlocking the building and outside gates before services. So, each Sunday I would open the doors to the building and the gates to the fence around the property.

As soon as I opened the outside gate of the church, a jeep came to an abrupt halt in front of me, and two security police jumped off the jeep and walked inside the gate. I shook their hands, welcomed them to our church, and invited them inside for the service. They refused. "We were sent here to take care of the security for the church during the service," they replied.

I explained, "We don't need security in the church, so we welcome you to come and join in our worship this Sunday." "No, no. We just came to do our job by taking care of the security for the church, and after you finish your service, we would like to meet with you," they responded.

Each guard went to one side of the gate and stood there with their AK-47 rifles. I thought, "How can the people come into the church with this kind of welcome?"

Most people rode bicycles or mopeds to church, since many people did not have cars in Vietnam during this time. People began arriving at church around 8:30 a.m. to be welcomed by two security police with AK-47s. When the men turned inside the gate, they quickly stopped, dropped off their wives, turned around and drove away.

The service started and as I looked at the congregation I got really worried. I had planned for the men who served as elders and deacons to come forward and share their testimony so that I would have a sermon, but they were not there. The only people in the congregation this morning were women. Now, what was I going to do for a sermon?

All of a sudden God brought to my mind the time I heard Dr.Cho share about the women ministering in his church in Korea. As I stood at the pulpit, God spoke to me about training women for the ministry. In the Vietnamese culture, women are not as valued as men. One example of this is women walking three steps behind their husbands, instead of by their sides.

God began to teach me as I stood there. In the letter Paul the Apostle sent to the church in Galatia, Paul mentioned that in Christ, there is no longer male or female. Through the blood of Jesus Christ, they are equal. I was reminded that when Christ was on the earth, the disciples were always around Him, but the women were far away and they only served.

However, when Christ was on the cross, there were more women with Him at death than there were men. When they placed Christ in the grave, the women were there. The women were also the first Christians who went out to preach the Good News that Jesus had risen. Through the women, the Gospel reached out to the whole world.

God spoke to me to equip and train the women for serving the Lord. As time would reveal, training women to do the work of the ministry became a strengthening factor for the Church of Vietnam. Under the Communists, many churches were closed; pastors were arrested and put into forced labor camps, re-education camps, jails and prisons.

The Assemblies of God also did not have any pastors left in Vietnam. The police were not as suspicious of the women, however, and the women had more courage than most of the men. As I preached the message that God had suddenly dropped in my spirit, the women said, "Amen, amen, and amen!"

After the service, the two security police approached me. "Sir, have you finished your service?" they asked."Yes, we just finished our service," I replied."Well, it's time for you to give us the key," they demanded. I was a little puzzled, "What key?" They were becoming annoyed, "The key to this building. We have come to take over this building!"

I answered, "Wow, you should have told me earlier, so that I could have my church vote. Since you just told me, why don't you come back next Sunday? I will have my church vote. If they want to give you the key, they can do that, but I cannot give you the key because the church doesn't belong to me." This seemed to satisfy them, so they left. I had a week to prepare my people before the officers returned the next Sunday.

I locked up the gates and the church building and went to bed that evening. As I reflected on the day, I was thankful that the Holy Spirit was with me and that He gave me a message to encourage the women. I still was not sure how to handle the situation with the police returning the following Sunday, but I knew God would give me the wisdom. I fell sound asleep. I was awakened by the noise of people yelling and the crashing of the gates and doors of the church. Suddenly, a large group of security officers broke through the door to my room, put me in handcuffs, and hauled me off to prison.

FIRST PRISON TERM

My first arrest was only one week after the communist takeover. The officers brought me to the top security prison in Saigon being used for politicians and spies.Each prisoner was assigned to their own cell, in order to prevent communication between prisoners. My cell was underground without windows, lights, or even a hint of light from the hallway. My daily meal consisted of one bowl of rice and a little salt.

I had been at this prison only a couple days when they brought me to an interrogation room with very bright lights. It was painful to go from total darkness to blinding light. As I sat in the interrogation chair, communist officials gathered around me to ask questions regarding my supposed involvement with the U.S. Central Intelligence Agency (CIA).

"What is your role in the CIA?" they asked. "What is your connection with American missionaries? Are ICI and CIA the same?" During the Vietnam War, the communists thought some missionaries were agents of the CIA, so naturally they were suspicious of anyone with possible connections to missionaries from the United States.

Since the acronyms "ICI" and "CIA" are similar, there was also suspicion that the International Correspondent Institute (ICI) of which I had been director was a part of the Central Intelligence Agency (CIA). They were convinced that I was a spy, and that speaking in tongues was a secret code for communicating with other spies.

After the interrogation, they returned me to my cell. This happened several times over the course of my internment at this prison. Each time, I was taken to the interrogation room and tortured with the light and the physical assault of the security officers. All of this was an effort to force me to admit to being a spy, whichthey realized was not the case eventually.

Entrance to the first prison I was held in Saigon

This was probably the most difficult of my prison terms. Naturally, I did not know what to expect, since this was my first time in prison. However, more difficult than not knowing what to expect was being in solitary confinement.

The only human contact outside of the hours of interrogation was when I was given my one bowl of rice and salt each day. It was more like being a caged animal, but even caged animals get to see light. I lost track of time, so I really do not know how long I was in this prison.

The only way to keep my spirit hopeful was to pray and worship, just as Paul and Silas did in the book of Acts in the New Testament. The more I prayed and worshiped, the more courage I gained. I could tell that the Holy Spirit was with me, and He gave me grace to endure. I also spent my time preaching out loud to myself in English, which is one thing that helped to prepare me for future ministry.

At one point I located a metal pipe in my cell and used it to talk with a colonel of the South Vietnamese secret service, who I learned was in a nearby cell. We had many conversations via water pipe, and I had the privilege to lead him to accept Jesus as his Savior. I did not realize it then, but even there the Lord was already demonstrating what He was going to do through my life and testimony.

After three months of being questioned, I was moved to another prison. Since I was not a spy and could not offer any helpful information, there was no need to keep me at the top security prison. I was still considered a threat, however, because I was a preacher, so they moved me to a political prison.

This prison had been used by the South Vietnamese government for political prisoners. Now it was being used by the communists as a prison for people they considered political dissenters. I was the youngest prisoner, and the only pastor.

People remained quiet at this prison because they did not know who they could trust. Oftentimes, the communists would infiltrate the prisoners with spies to try to get information. As a result, people were very hesitant to talk. Of course, I did not have anything to hide, so I shared my testimony every day. A lot of people did not believe me and did not trust me because my story did not make sense to them, but they did believe when they saw signs, wonders and miracles done.

I prayed for the sick to be healed, and they were healed. People saw that I lived in peace, and as I prayed for others they had peace, as well. I had private altar calls to receive the Lord, because people were afraid of the spies in their midst.

In September 1975, I was moved to a forced labor camp in Quan Chim, a secret area in what was called a "new economic zone." The living conditions at this camp were terrible. We were forcedinto hard labor clearing forests and starting farms. We were allowed very little food from the crops because it all belonged to the government.

My prison cell was a steel container, so every night I was caged in the container until the next morning when it was time to go to the fields to work. The prisoners were treated like animals because they were considered of less worth than even a cow or buffalo. I had no sugar, no toothpaste, and no new clothes over four years.

At the end of 1979, I was supposed to move to another prison camp. However, one of the prison guards told me, "Pastor Ai, you don't know who I am, but I know who you are. You helped my family move from central to South Vietnam, and we really appreciate what you did. So, I want to help you."

He went on to explain a plan that would allow me to escape from the forced labor camp. "I will come to your container to check on you around 11:00 tonight. Ask me to allow you to use the toilet. When I lock you back in your container, I will fix the lock so that it is not tight. About half an hour later you should just put your hat down and your shoes and arrange your pillow like you are sleeping. Then, you can remove the lock and get out."

He showed me the way that I should escape without being detected, and he described where to go when I reached the woods. So when the guard checked on me at 11:00, I did just as he said. A half hour later, I was able to escape undetected; and just after midnight, two pastors met me in the forest. They helped me get to safety in another province.

Later on, I tried to locate the man who helped me escape from the labor camp. I contacted everyone that I remembered helping move from central Vietnam to the South, but no one had any family members that would fit his description. To this day, I have not learned who he was. I can only imagine that it was an angel sent to rescue me, just like Peter was rescued from prison in the New Testament.

A WAY OF LIFE

The threat and reality of arrest and imprisonment became a normal way of life for me after my first experience in 1975-1979. The communist Vietnamese government considered me a political dissenter and a threat to communism, so I was frequently arrested and sentenced anywhere from a couple of days to six months in prison or forced labor camps.

Often, when news leaked out to the world that I had been arrested and put in prison, the communist government released me from prison and kept me under house arrest. In the early nineties, I was sentenced to three terms in a re-education camp, a total of nine years.

Since I could be arrested at any time, I learned to always be prepared. In the prisons in Vietnam, you have to bring your own soap, toothbrush, toothpaste and other personal items, or your family has to bring them to you. After my first experience in prison and labor camp, I decided to carry a backpack with the essential personal items I would need if sent to prison again.

I carried this bag with me everywhere I went. It stayed next to me even when I was sleeping at home. When I was awakened by the dogs barking at night, I would check to be sure my bag was still with me. I never knew when the police would come to arrest me. Of course I did not want to go to prison, but God had a plan with each of my imprisonments, and I was able to lead hundreds and then thousands of people to the Lord, even in the midst of the worst conditions.

Many churches were started in the prisons and labor camps, and many prisoners went on to become pastors and leaders in the churches in prison and then in their villages when they were released from prison.

I considered it exciting because of the challenge of being a witness and leading others to the Lord. I was able to minister to people that would have never stepped foot in a church. My message was always about a new heart and a new life. They called me "radical for Jesus." Some of the people I led to the Lord had been the top gangsters and the toughest prisoners.

Even the police saw the good that I did and were able to hear the message of hope. They were often scared of me because I refused to answer their questions until they answered mine. I turned their accusations and their questions around to talk to them, and to preach to them.

The threat of arrest and imprisonment was also taxing on my family. My wife, Ruth, never knew whether I would be at home or on my way to prison when she returned from running errands or from ministering.In the late nineties, my children were denied education in the schools because I was considered "worse than a criminal."

One day neither my wife nor I were able to pick up my oldest daughter, Baby Ruth, from school. The police had come to arrest me, and they were interrogating me and searching our house. They did not allow anyone to leave to get Ruth from school.

The teacher called our house at 6:00 in the evening and was greeted by the police from our telephone. They refused to allow us to talk with her. They commanded that the teacher bring Ruth home. By the time that the teacher dropped Baby Ruth home, many of the neighborhood kids had gathered near our house. "Oh, poor Ruth, your dad was taken away by the police!"

Baby Ruth was wondering what was going on. Of course, she knew I was arrested a lot, but she did not know why the police came to arrest me this time. My wife always explained to Baby Ruth that we were hated by the police because we preach the Gospel.

The next morning when Ruth went to school, her teacher told her to go to the principal's office. The principal told her, "Sorry, Ruth, according to the police report, your dad was arrested and put in jail, so you can no longer go to school."

Baby Ruth began to cry, "Why?" "Well, according to the police, your dad is a bad guy. That's why they put him in prison," the principal said to her. "No, no, my dad is a good guy. I know that he helps people," Ruth told her.

"We don't know what he does. We only know that the police have said that he is a bad guy. That is why you cannot be in this school anymore," the principal explained.

Ruth asked, "Why? Other students are in the school whose fathers are criminals because they committed a crime. My dad is not a criminal. He is a pastor. He does good things."

The principal told Baby Ruth, "You know what, girl, criminals can only harm one or two people. According to the police, what your dad is doing is harming a whole generation." Baby Ruth walked home, thinking to herself, "If my dad can harm a whole generation by the good things he does, I want to be like him."

A year later she went to summer camp where she made her decision to follow Jesus, and to follow in her father's footsteps to become a preacher. Later, she went on to Bible college to serve the Lord.

My children were denied schooling that even the children of criminals could receive because I was considered worse than a criminal. The government believed that I was harming a whole generation by leading them to the Lord and that the result would be that they would turn away from communism.

ARREST IN SAIGON

When I was arrested in Saigon after returning from Cambodia in February 1991, our Bible school was two years old, and I was the General Superintendent of the Assemblies of God in Vietnam. Ruth and I traveled extensively to evangelize, disciple people and start churches. Our ministry was going well. God was really growing His Church in Vietnam. We were discipling new converts and training new pastors to start churches.

This arrest in Saigon was nothing new for me, so I knew that it was time to reach more prisoners for Christ. This time I was sentenced without a trial to a total of nine years in prison, forced labor camp, and re-education camp. I was taken to Phan Dang Luu prison where I was placed in a suffocating, hot, small prison cell with sixty other prisoners. The cell had a steel roof and only one door, and no window. At times it became so hot that we had to strip down and stand still just to stay as cool as possible.

In spite of the conditions, I was glad that I had an opportunity to share my testimony with people. It took a while for people to believe that I was a pastor, though. They could not understand that a pastor would be in prison, and that a pastor would have half his body covered in tattoos. They first suspected that I was sent by the government to spy on them to get information from those prisoners who had been high officials in the South Vietnamese government.

After they heard my story and saw the treatment I received from the security guards, they realized that I was not a spy and were open to listen to the good news of Jesus. Though it started going well with the prisoners, each day I faced hours of interrogation by the security officers.

It was the same line of questioning that happened every time I had been arrested over the previous fifteen years: "What are you doing preaching, teaching, evangelizing? Are you connected with the U.S. government? What is your connection with the CIA?"

They thought that I was trained and funded by the CIA because I kept preaching and teaching, even though I kept being arrested. Their reasoning was that I must be funded by the American government, or else I would have stopped. They considered me a political dissenter, and they were afraid that I was rallying people to turn against the government. They did not realize that the more Vietnamese people love Jesus and serve Him, the more peaceful and prosperous Vietnam would become.

I became good at interacting with my interrogators. If they wanted an answer from me, then they would have to answer some of my questions, first. I realized that this was the only way that some of them would ever hear the Gospel, and God had trusted me enough to allow me to bring the Gospel message to them.

It was a challenge to turn their questioning into a rational discussion and to share the message of salvation. Through it all, the Holy Spirit gave me wisdom and direction in my conversation, and these officers came face-to-face with the reality of their need for salvation.

KING PRISONER

In September 1991, I was transferred from Phan Dang Luu to Chi Hoa, the largest prison in Saigon. It houses 10,000 prisoners and is considered the worst prison in Saigon.

It was built in 1940 by the Japanese when they invaded Vietnam. The communist regime was using the prison for criminals they considered needed maximum security, including people with life sentences or death sentences. In this prison, I continued to share my testimony and lead people to the Lord, and there were many miracles that happened. One miracle had to do with tithing.

The government provided prisoners with only four liters of water each day for everything they must do – washing and drinking. The fact is that the gangs in the prison controlled the waterso each prisoner really only received one liter of water each day.

When I came to the prison I led the gangsters to the Lord, and I began teaching them to live in faith and justice. I explained that they should not keep the extra water for themselves; they should allow each person to have their four liters each day. They agreed, and soon they began allowing everyone to have their full rationed amount.

Entrance to Chi Hoa in Saigon

Next, I began teaching them about tithing. They said, "Pastor, you must be kidding us! We don't have anything to give to the Lord in this prison. So, how can you teach us about giving?" Another guy laughed and said, "If we give, we only have water to give!"

God began dealing with their hearts and they eventually asked, "All we have is water. Can we give water?"I said, "Yes. Jesus said in the Bible that whoever gives a glass of water to an apostle will be rewarded as an apostle. So, it's as important as anything else."

They responded, "Okay, if you're serious, we'll assign one guy who will be in charge of the water. Then, every day when the prisoners receive four liters of water, they will give ten percent of it to you."When they began tithing their water, I had 20 – 30 liters of water each day, so they gave me the title, "King Prisoner."

One of the problems in this prison was that nearly every prisoner had some type of skin disease. The authorities came to investigate the causes of this and discovered that it was due to lack of vitamins and adequate amounts of calories through food. The greatest cause, however, was a lack of water for bathing and drinking. They decided that the prison needed more water, so the plan was to build tanks that would be filled during the night to provide enough water for the prisoners during the day.

When the tanks were built, they were put into our room. We now had all the water that we needed!I explained, "Look, only one month after you started tithing, God has performed a miracle. He has provided us with more than enough water for our needs!" This was a great testimony to the power and provision of God.

PROSTITUTES' PRISON

The government had put me into a political prison and it did not change me. They had put me into a criminal prison and it did not change me.

So in March 1993, they transferred me to Tong Le Cham, a prostitutes' prison near the border of Cambodia. They thought this would ruin me as a pastor, and then they would not have any more trouble out of me. The women hated me because I did not succumb to them. I resolved to show the love of Jesus to them, no matter what they did. It is the kindness of God that leads us to have a repentant heart and to accept the love of Christ.

I also knew the Bible says that God will be with us wherever we go and whenever we need Him (see Joshua 1:9), so I prayed, "Lord, I declare that You will be with me. You are Emmanuel. I need You to help me lead these women to You."

It was tough. Each time I began to tell them my testimony and how much Jesus loved them, they made fun of me. They did not want to hear any of it. "Shut up! We don't believe you. We don't care what you have to say. We need your love, not Jesus." One day they challenged me, "If your Jesus really loves us, then you can do what we say. Your job is to clean all the toilets."

The toilets in the prison were not clean ceramic commodes that are flushed to dispose of wastes. These toilets were big barrels covered with a board that had a small hole cut into it and a bamboo pole on each side of the hole for balance. We had to squat on top of the barrel and balance ourselves on the two poles to "do our business."

My job was to take out all of the waste from the barrels each day with my bare hands, put it into buckets to mix with water, and then fertilize the vegetables in the field. The stench was humanly unbearable and the sight was nauseating. That was my job though, and I could only pray that God would use this for His glory. If the prostitutes could see an example of the true love of God through me doing this, then it would be worth the intolerable discomfort. Only the love and grace of God strengthened me to do this with a loving heart and gracious attitude.

The women watched me and laughed, "Oh, look at Pastor Ai, now. He is so dirty. Look at what he has to do!"I responded, "Ladies, listen, nothing outside is dirty. When Jesus was on earth, He told the Pharisees, 'Nothing outside is dirty, but the things in your mind and in your heart are dirty.' Many times He said to them, 'Be careful, you Pharisees, the tax collectors and the prostitutes will go into heaven before you.'"

The women were surprised. "What, Pastor Ai, are you kidding? The prostitutes will go to heaven?" This was shocking to them. In Vietnamese culture, if a woman becomes a prostitute she has no more future. It means that her life is over; she is as good as dead. I went on to tell them about Rahab, a prostitute mentioned in the book of Joshua in the Bible. I explained how God used her to bring liberation to an entire nation. I also described to them several women leaders in our churches who had been prostitutes. God had changed them and now they were serving the Lord in ministry.

As soon as I mentioned the name of one lady who had become an evangelist, they exclaimed, "Wow, we know her. She was our boss!" I told them, "You know what? She is my disciple, and she is a wonderful soul winner."

They wanted to hear her story, so I continued, "We have a lot of women ministers who have been put into prison for preaching the Gospel. When they are in prison, they have the opportunity to share the good news of Jesus with other prisoners.""One of our women ministers was in prison and led your former boss to the Lord and discipled her. God changed her life. When she got out of prison, she went to Bible school. After Bible school, she became a soul winner and an evangelist."

They were amazed and asked, "How did this happen?" I asked, "Well, do you want to hear another story?" They told me, "Pastor Ai, just wash your hands and then tell us more stories."I cleaned up and then continued, "People look on the outside, but God looks on the inside.""This is why the Bible tells us that whoever is in Christ becomes a new creation. All old things are passed away, and everything becomes new in Jesus Christ." (*See II Corinthians 5:17.*)

I told them story after story of how God changed prostitutes and others from old into new. I said, "You know, when you become a Christian, the blood of Jesus Christ cleans you from all of your sin and when God looks at you, He sees you through Jesus. He no longer sees you as a prostitute. You are a new creation in Christ."

As they listened to these miraculous accounts and to the truth of salvation, tears began to run down their faces. They asked me, "Pastor Ai, is there any hope for us?" I said, "Yes, that is why God sent me here!"

One by one, many of the women began to accept Jesus as their Savior and a transformation took place in them individually and then affected the entire prison. Before they surrendered their lives to the Lord, their language, conversations, and actions were vulgar. Female police officers were sent to the prison to re-educate and train the women prisoners. The prostitutes had so much influence that the female police officers began to talk like them and even act like them.

After the prostitutes surrendered their lives to the Lord, there was a noticeable change in their language and conduct. The prison became a model prison, and thousands of prisoners were sent from all over Vietnam to be rehabilitated at this prison. The government did not know where to send me next! They thought sending me to this prostitutes' prison would change me.

Instead, God, through me, changed the prison. I was only at Tong Le Cham a short time when, at the request of Francois Mitterrand, president of France at the time, I was released in 1993. I returned home and continued preaching the Gospel and starting churches.

HANOI HILTON

In May 1999, I was conducting Bible school classes in Hanoi. Ironically, we had class in the hotel across from the security police station. A couple days into the training, the security police arrested me and took me to the infamous prison, Hanoi Hilton.

The interrogation I experienced at this prison was the worst I had experienced to that point. Since I was the General Superintendent of the Assemblies of God in Vietnam, they brought in the generals of the security police to interrogate me. They thought I was too young and too funny to be a "general." Even in the midst of interrogation, I kept my sense of humor which irritated them even more.

They questioned me for four weeks, fifteen to eighteen hours each day. It was mentally exhausting to keep up with their lines of questioning. I had to remember what they were asking me and figure out how it fit with everything else so that I would not mistakenly give them information that would put someone else in danger.

I also learned that they had plans to kill me. With the mental exhaustion and the sweltering heat, my body wore down and I fainted. When I came to, I was incoherent and I could not move. They took me to a government hospital, but they did not have the medicine to give me that I needed. By this time news of my imprisonment had spread around the world and Christians began to pray. A group from Canada visited my wife in Saigon to encourage her and let her know that they were writing a story that would let more people know of my imprisonment.

The Vietnamese government was getting a lot of social and political pressure to release me, so when I became ill they allowed me to hire two private doctors and to get a room in the hotel across the street. In the morning I had a doctor attend to me that practiced western medicine. In the afternoon I had a doctor attend to me that practiced Chinese medicine.

Once I was well enough to travel, my wife was allowed to fly from Saigon to Hanoi to pay the doctors' and hotel bills and take me home. I still was not free. We were constantly followed by the police to ensure that I did not carry on any further "illegal activities," and once at home I was under house arrest. At the news of this imprisonment, arrangements started being made to request religious asylum in the U.S., and in December 1999 my family and I emigrated to the U.S.

BROTHER HEN

I met Hen when he came to Tong Le Cham prison. He was one of the ten thousand prisoners that were being sent to the prison. The government declared Tong Le Cham a model prison as a result of these changes in prisoners' behavior. What the government did not recognize was that the change was a result of the former prostitutes giving their hearts to the Lord, rather than any work being done by the security officers that had been assigned to that prison. Nevertheless, God used this as an opportunity to bring more people to hear the Gospel, including Hen.

In Vietnam, prisoners received food from family members who would bring a basket of food to them in prison. If family or friends did not bring any food, then a prisoner was limited to what someone would share with them, to the meager rice porridge at the prison, or worse yet, no food at all.

I befriended Hen and started sharing my food with him. I began to learn that he was from northern Vietnam, 2,000 miles away. This explained why he did not have anyone to bring him any food. It also explained why he had trouble communicating with other people. He was from one of the Montagnard tribes, so his dialect was very different.

He had been arrested and accused of being a spy, and he was sentenced to life in prison without receiving a trial. When I met him, he had already been a prisoner for six years and had been through several different prisons. It was a while before I was able to share my testimony with Hen, mainly because it was difficult to talk with him.

Eventually, though, I was able to lead him to accept Jesus as his Savior. I told him, "God saved you, and He has a great plan for your life to bring the Good News back to your family and your village." He was not really sure about this, but I encouraged him. After his conversion I was sure to train him to understand the basic truths of God's Word and to begin growing in the Lord. I told him, "God will bring you out of prison so that you can study at my Bible school and then go back to your people and your village."

Two months later, I was released from prison. Hen was very happy for me but sad for himself. I assured him that I would come to visit him and bring him food. If I was not able to come, then I would send another pastor to meet him. I also told him that I would pray for him to be released. He reminded me that he was supposed to serve life in prison with no chance of parole, but I assured him that the power of God was greater than any decree that the government had established. I told him, "If it is God's will for you to be released from prison, then it will happen."

I was released from prison with a stern warning not to continue preaching and training. I returned to my home in Saigon, and I continued preaching and training. Three months later my family and I were preparing to sit down for dinner and there was a knock at the door. My wife opened the door and was shocked to see Brother Hen standing there. She recognized him because she used to bring food to both of us while I was in prison.

"Honey, come here! Brother Hen is here!" she called out to me. I was nervous when I heard this because he was supposed to be serving life in prison. My first thought was that he had escaped from prison. The Montagnard people are known for being very good at escaping from prison and surviving in the jungle. I also wondered whether the government had made a deal with him: allow him to run away and come see me so that they would have a reason to arrest me.

I was happy to see him, but I asked, "Brother Hen, what are you doing here?" "Pastor Ai, praise the Lord! God answered our prayers!" he told me excitedly. "What do you mean?" I asked. "I'm free! They released me from prison," he explained. He was insistent that they had released him.

What concerned me now was that the government had made a deal with him: allow him to leave without a certificate of release, but he had to come visit me. This would be a way to trap me.

If I allowed him to stay with us and he did not have formal permission to leave, then I could be arrested for harboring a fugitive. This, compounded with continuing to preach and teach, would certainly mean a long prison term for me.

"Are you sure you've been released? Can I see your release certificate?" I asked.He looked at me funny and said, "Pastor Ai, didn't you pray for me? Why do you not believe that God answered your prayers?" "Well, yes I believe, but I have to make sure. When they released me from prison they told me, 'Don't preach, teach or release any more people into the ministry; otherwise, you will be back to prison.'

"I told them, 'A water buffalo was made to plow the field; a horse was made to pull the cart; and a preacher was made to preach the Gospel. What can I do I was made to be a preacher?' "They said, 'We will put you back in prison again.' "I told them, 'Well, you do your job, and I will do my job.'

"So, when I do my job I have to be very careful, or they will find a way to put me back into prison. That is why I need to see your release certificate.'"Pastor Ai, I'm sorry that you prayed and you don't believe that God answered, but here is my release certificate," Brother Hen said as he handed me a piece of paper.

I carefully read the paper and realized that this was not a trick from the government; it was a miracle from God. Brother Hen had been released from a life sentence in prison! I invited him to eat dinner with us.

We shared and talked for a while, and then I asked him, "Brother Hen, when will you go back to your village?" "Well, it will take about five days and five nights to get back to my village, since it is near the border with China. The police told me that I have five days and five nights before I have to check in at the police station. But I am not going to do that, Pastor Ai."

"No? Why? What are you going to do?" I asked."I want to go to your Bible school," he said.I tried to reason with him, "I don't think this is a good time for you to do that. Why don't you go back to your town and check in at the police station? Then you can come back to go to Bible school."

"No, Pastor Ai. If I do that, they will put me under house arrest, and I will not be able to go anywhere. I need to go to Bible school because I need to learn the Word of God, so that I can bring the hope back to my village, just as you told me when I was converted," he insisted.

"Brother Hen, we need to really talk about this. I don't want you to go to my Bible school, get arrested, and then the police blame me that I was the one who demanded that you go to Bible school."

"Pastor Ai, I am old enough, and I can take responsibility for myself. Just put me in your Bible school. If I am arrested, I will tell them that I volunteered to do it, and that you did not make me."

I finally agreed. Brother Hen spent the next month being trained as a soul winner, the "Caleb" level. People complete the training for this level in one month. After the training, they must go back to their villages or towns for one month and practice what they learned. They are required to read the Bible through one time and lead five people to the Lord.

I paid the fare for Brother Hen to return to his village, and gave him instructions to call me when he had finished the requirements. I would send a pastor to baptize the people that he led to the Lord. We would also make plans for him to come back for the "Joshua" level, so he could train to be a cell leader.

A month later the phone rang and it was Brother Hen. "Pastor Ai, I walked 60 kilometers to the nearest phone so that I could report to you. It is exactly 30 days from when I left you."

"Great! Tell me how things are going for you." I told him."Pastor Ai, could you send me a pastor?" he asked."What for?" I asked."For water baptism," he replied."Brother Hen, do you have five souls ready to be baptized?""No, sir. Pastor Ai, please send a pastor…"

"Brother Hen, listen, why are you asking me for a pastor without five souls to be baptized? You know the qualification is to win five souls and to read the Bible through one time.""Pastor Ai, you just cut me off. You did not let me finish. I do not have five souls, but I do have five villages."I was surprised when I heard this. "Brother Hen, how many souls altogether?"

"Pastor Ai, believe me, I have tried my very best. The security in my village is very tight. I cannot leave my home. I was only able to lead 753 people to the Lord."I was not sure what I heard him say, "How many people altogether, Brother Hen?"

A little embarrassed, he replied, "Pastor Ai, please understand, I tried my best, but in the last thirty days, I could only lead 753 people to the Lord.""Wow, 753 people! Praise the Lord, Brother Hen! Well, I cannot leave right away, but I will send a pastor. I will come as soon as I can."

The next day I sent a pastor to Brother Hen's area to baptize people and to start a church. I rearranged my calendar and a month later I was able to join them.

Brother Hen was excited when he saw me. "Pastor Ai, you came all the way from Saigon to visit me! It is a long way.""Brother Hen, I wanted to visit you, to get to know your parents, your family, and your people. I also want to learn from you how you led 753 people to the Lord in one month."

He looked at me, "Pastor Ai, it's easy. I just did what you taught me in Bible school."I told him, "I realize that, but a lot of people say the same thing. I want to learn what you did.""Pastor Ai, I promise you. I did not do anything wrong. I did exactly what you taught me. Pastor Ai, if anything is wrong, it is your fault; it is not my fault!"

"Okay, just tell me what is going on," I told him. "Well, Pastor Ai, you know you made a big mistake," he started. "How do you mean? What mistake did I make?" I asked him.

"Well, when I got back to my village, my brother was very sick. He had been sick for six months and was about to die. Everyone was excited when I arrived. They thanked the gods that I had come home. They thought the gods had brought me home just in time to see my brother before he died."

"I told them, 'No my God sent me home not to prepare to bury him, but to bring good news.' "I invited everyone to come into the house, and I began to explain that Jesus died on the cross for us."

"When Jesus hung on the cross for us, He bore all of our sickness, so don't worry about sickness. I will read some good news to you from Mark 16, James 5, and Isaiah 53 in the Bible. Then I will do my job, you do your job, and God will do His job."

"I turned to my brother and said, 'Since you are sick, James chapter 5 says to invite your elders to come, confess your sins, and have them lay hands on you, anoint you and pray, and God will take care of the rest.' I turned to my family and said, 'Since I have been a Christian for five months, I am the elder of this family, so just listen to me. I will lead you to repent of your sins.'"

"So I led the whole family into a prayer of repentance and to accept Jesus as their Lord and Savior. I turned to my brother again, 'Now as the elder, I not only led you in the prayer of repentance, but now I will anoint you with oil, lay hands on you, and pray in Jesus' name for you to be healed.'"

"That's when I thought, 'Uh-oh, Pastor Ai made a big mistake. He taught me, trained me, sent me home, but he did not give me any holy oil to bring home.' I checked with my mom and we only had cooking oil and lamp oil. 'Which one is better?' I asked my mom. 'They're both good,' she told me."

"I was really unsure what to do. I thought you had made a very big mistake by not giving me any holy oil to bring home. All I had was cooking oil and lamp oil. How could I anoint my brother and pray for him?"

Pastor Hen's brother, me, Brother Hen

"Suddenly the Holy Spirit said to me, 'Don't worry.' He reminded me of Jesus turning the water into wine at the wedding of Cana. I prayed, 'Jesus, since you are Emmanuel God, You are with me everywhere. When you were at the wedding of Cana, You turned the water into wine, so I believe that You can turn cooking oil and lamp oil into holy oil.'"

"I asked my mother to bring a bowl of each of them, and I prayed that God would turn one of them into holy oil. Since I didn't know which one He turned into holy oil, I dipped one finger into the cooking oil and one finger into the lamp oil and anointed my brother."

"After I prayed, I told everyone, 'Okay, we have done our job, now we wait for God to do His job.' So we all went to bed. The next morning, I was awakened by an old man in our neighborhood demanding to know what had happened."

"When my brother woke up that morning he was very hot, so he got up and walked slowly out to the front yard to take a bath. After he bathed, he started helping my mother wash his clothes that he had been wearing for a long time. The old man was walking to our house and saw my brother. He said, 'What? Are you still alive?!'"

"My brother said, 'Yes, sir, I am still alive!' The old man said, 'What was all the noise last night? I thought you had died. I came by this morning to help with the burial.' He described hearing all the noise the night before and thought that my brother had died, so he was coming to help with the burial. Instead, he saw my brother was very much alive!"

"My brother explained what happened, 'The noise that you heard last night was because my family was excited that Hen came home from prison.'"

"The old man was astounded, 'Do you mean that your brother who is serving life in prison escaped from prison and came home?!'"

"'No his God sent him home with good news for us. Last night he read something in a Book, and then he put oil on my head and laid hands on me and he spoke in a strange language that he learned in prison, but there is more. Why don't you talk to him and ask him?' my brother told him."

"That is when the old man woke me up and demanded that I tell him what happened. I opened the Bible to the scriptures that I read the night before and explained everything to him. He then asked, 'Can you do the same thing one more time? My youngest son has the same sickness.'"

"I told him, 'No problem. Just gather your whole family and bring your son here.' When the old man brought his family and his sick son, I opened the Bible to Mark 16, James 5, and Isaiah 53 and described how God performs miracles. I led them in repentance and prayed for his son, and God healed him."

"The news about what God had done quickly spread through our village and the surrounding villages. Pastor Ai, for thirty days I was not able to leave my home. There were so many people who kept coming to be healed. That is how I led 753 people to the Lord in 30 days."

It was amazing and encouraging to hear the account of what God had done through Brother Hen. We sent twelve people to train the new believers for one-and-a-half months. At the ceremony celebrating the completion of this training, Hen was arrested and sentenced to prison for four years. This did not stop him, though.

He started a church in the first prison, so he was moved to another prison. He started a church in that prison, so they moved him to another prison. Each time he started a church, he was moved to another prison. He started four churches in four years in four separate prisons.Hen returned to his village after four years of prison, and the church had grown ten times what it was when it was started four years prior. God blessed Brother Hen and used him to spread the Gospel to the northwest part of Vietnam.

THE BACKPACK

As I mentioned earlier, my first term in prison taught me that I needed to bring my own toothbrush, toothpaste, underwear and other personal items with me. These things were not provided for the prisoners.

Realizing that I would likely be arrested again, I decided to pack a simple bag with essentials for staying in prison. This bag went with me everywhere so that I would have it if I was arrested.

I really wanted to use a backpack rather than the bag, but there were not any backpacks available. In 1988 a short-term missions group from the Philippines came to Vietnam. One of the ladies on the team whose name was Susan blessed me with a backpack. From 1988 on, I used the backpack instead of my other bag.

When I was arrested in 1990 the backpack went with me to the forced labor camp. The guards allowed me to keep it, but they cut the straps for fear I would use them to hang myself. They also stamped "CT" on it. In Vietnamese, CT stands for re-education, but we can also do a word play on it that

The backpack, hat, and folded uniform

means child of God. So, the guards were actually helping me spread the good news of being a child of God!

In this labor camp we were forced to work ten to twelve hours every day on the rubber plantation, cashew, nut and potato farms. It was not easy to carry the backpack without any straps, so I really wanted it to be fixed.One of the toughest prisoners there was nick-named "Scissor." He was a tailor by trade, but he was in prison for stabbing people to death with scissors.

Even in prison he carried scissors as a weapon, and He had a reputation for killing people with them. Everyone was his enemy, and even the guards were afraid of him. He was also afraid of other people wanting to kill him, so he wore a breastplate made out of metal cans to keep from being stabbed to death.I began to share the love of Jesus with Scissor and told him how Jesus would give him peace and be his friend. As I continued to show him friendship and God's grace, he gave his heart to the Lord. I was able to bring reconciliation between him and the other prisoners for God's glory.

As an expression of gratitude, Scissor used one of his shirts to fix the straps for my backpack and to make a hat for me to protect my head from the sun. Even though both of these things were against the rules of the prison, Scissor said, "If the guards ask you where you got these, just tell them they are from me, and you will be safe." The Lord used Scissor to bless me with not only the backpack and hat, but also protection.

THE UNIFORM

Usually when people are put into prison they are so filled with fear and worry that their hair turns white and they get very thin because there is such little food. Since this happens, the prison uniforms are only made very small. The only food a prisoner receives is what his family or friends bring him to eat. When I was in prison in 1990, my wife was not allowed to bring me food for the first month. All I was allowed to eat was some rice with a little salt given to me by the other prisoners.

Every day for twelve hours the police would interrogate me. After the interrogation, I would return to my cell, eat a little rice and go right to sleep. This would cause anxiety and depression for most people, but I was at peace. Even though the cell was very small, and sometimes there were 70 of us crammed into the cell at one time, I was able to sleep soundly. I also gained weight, instead of losing it. The officers were amazed and wondered how it could happen. They could not understand how I could be in a state of perfect peace.

I knew the Lord had sent me there to minister to the prisoners and to the police. So for the twelve hours that the police were questioning me every day, I would preach the Gospel to them. Because of my testimony and witness, I gained the respect of the officers.

One of the officers personally provided me with bigger clothes since there were no uniforms large enough for me. He even allowed me to sew my initials on the shirt. This was the first time that this had ever been done for a prisoner.

OFFICER'S SANDALS

When I was in prison in 1991, I met a man who had been an Army Major in the North Vietnamese army. After Saigon fell to the communists in 1975, he was offered a high position in the government. He became corrupt, so now he was in prison. When he was arrested, he was stripped of everything, his rank, medals, and uniform.

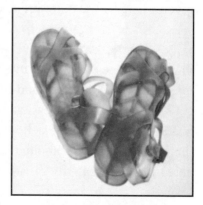

Sandals issued to high-ranking officials of North Vietnamese army

They wanted to take his sandals, but he begged to keep them. These sandals were only issued to high-ranking army officers in the North Vietnamese army. The sandals were made of rubber and were very nice compared to the sandals made from rubber tires that were issued to low-ranking officers. He wanted to keep the sandals so that everyone in prison would recognize that he had been a high ranking officer.

I had the opportunity to share my testimony and the message of the Gospel with him, and he received Jesus as his Lord and Savior. Shortly after he became a Christian, he gave me his sandals as not only a gift of appreciation, but as an offering to the Lord. He was giving up the pride of his past because he considered himself nothing before Christ. I wore the sandals in prison as a testimony to others, and people's hearts were opened to receive the Gospel.

THE BOX

Of course I had no Bible when I was in prison, but I wanted to have something that I could use to tell other prisoners about their need for the Lord. So I took a piece of wood from an old broken wardrobe that the police had

My "Bible" I carved from wood while in prison

thrown away. I began to file it on the ground to make it smooth. I found an old US Army boot that had a piece of metal in it and used the metal to make hinges for the box. I then used a piece of shrapnel to carve a cross on the outside of the box. I found a small mirror and used sticky rice to glue the mirror to the inside.

As I began to share the love of Jesus with prisoners, I would open the box as I would have opened a Bible, if I had one. The prisoners would look inside the box and see themselves in the mirror. This was as if they were looking into God's Word to see their own spiritual condition. They recognized their need for a Savior, and I would lead them to give their hearts to the Lord.

_____

After I escaped from the forced labor camp in 1979, I traveled and spoke in different churches to the youth. I kept crossing paths with a young woman who was traveling to various churches to minister to the children. Eventually, we were speaking at the same time at the same church.

Even though we had seen each other several times before, we had never really talked. Through the help of one of the pastors, however, we met and began to talk. Here, I want to have Ruth share her testimony and the story of how God brought us together.

RUTH AI'S TESTIMONY

I was raised in the city of Saigon. My parents were strong Christians who taught me a lot about the Bible, to love other people, and to share the good news of Jesus. In church, I really excelled in Sunday school, and received many recognitions and awards for my knowledge about the Bible.

I knew a lot about God, Jesus, the Bible and Christianity, and I was a good girl, but I did not have a relationship with Jesus. I was focused on the religion of being a Christian, instead of having a relationship with Jesus.

Ruth Ai in traditional costume

When I was 17 years old, I accepted Jesus as my personal Lord and Savior, and was baptized in water to show my decision to follow Jesus. One evening during a youth prayer meeting, God poured out His Spirit on about 20 of us. We were convicted and moved by the Holy Spirit that we all cried and repented before the Lord for over 2 hours. That night, in my heart I knew that God had called me to serve Him in full-time ministry, but I still did not completely surrender.

God reminded me of what He told Jeremiah, *"Before I formed you in the womb, I knew you; before you were born I set you apart. I appointed you as a prophet to the nations...."* (Jeremiah 1:4-5)Before the communists took over in 1975, I taught in a Christian school. I began to have a burden for my students because they were not Christians, so I went to the Lord in prayer and asked Him what I could do.

He told me to teach them about the Good News. After that, I always took the opportunity to share the love of God with my students and to take them to church. I led many of them to the Lord. I had this freedom to teach my students about Christ for about three years before the communist government took over and sent us to seminars to retrain us about evolution and atheism. Now, we were no longer permitted to teach about creation. The Holy Spirit in me did not agree with this, so I quit teaching.

God spoke to my heart about Samuel in the Bible. He said, "I have called you three times, but you have not answered Me." The Lord also brought two songs to me: "I Surrender All" and "I Don't Know About Tomorrow, But I Know Who Holds My Hand." That night on my knees I surrendered all of my heart and life to the Lord. I had lost everything, but I had won Jesus Christ. He impressed on my heart to go to Bible school for one year, but I did not know how I could pay for the tuition.

However, by selling all of my jewelry and with the help of a sponsor, I was able to go to Bible School for one year. Then the Communists took over the Bible School. I had gone to Bible School to learn more about Jesus and I did. Afterwards, I went back home to my parents and worked different jobs for several years, but I did not feel fulfilled in these jobs. I worked in a local church teaching children's Sunday school. Then, I served as a youth pastor.

At the time, I wasn't interested in dating but because I was serving as a youth pastor, some of the young men became interested in me.One man in particular wanted to marry me. I prayed to the Lord about this, but God did not answer, so we simply stayed friends.I began to pray for a husband. I told God, "If You want me to marry, please send me a husband that will be stronger in faith than I am so He can strengthen me when I am weak. Even if he lives in the countryside, I am willing to go with him." In Vietnam, the life of a person who lives in the city is very different from someone who lives in the country. City life is easier.

I dreamed and I prayed that I would meet a man who was strong in his faith, stronger than I was so that he would be able to help me. I forgot about the prayer, and I continued to work in ministry.At times, I traveled to different churches for children and youth ministry. When I was on one of these trips, I met a "crazy preacher".

We talked and fellowshipped, but we didn't think we would see each other again. When I was teaching the children in the courtyard, something happened in my mind, and I stopped and glanced over my shoulder. Oh-oh, I saw that there was a man watching me; it was Pastor Ai. I was so surprised to see him looking at me.

After I finished teaching the children, my pastor invited me to have lunch and again I met the "crazy preacher." He had spoken to the youth group in this same church. After dinner, it began to rain harder and harder, and we were not able to leave the church, so we had time to share about our ministries and our visions. By the end of the evening, we found out that we had fallen in love.

According to Vietnamese tradition, the man has to meet the woman's parents. While my parents were talking with him, they realized that he was the person they had heard about called the "crazy preacher."They told him,"Our daughter is a crazy teacher and if she is going to marry a crazy preacher like you, you will become "double crazy" and you will be in big trouble!"

Paul replied,"The whole world is crazy anyway. We would rather be crazy for the Lord, for eternity, than crazy for the world and go to hell."We were engaged for 6 months and were married in Saigon on June 1, 1980. I moved to the countryside with Paul to start a church.

There were only four members when we started this church, and at first the church grew slowly. Life was hard the first year, especially since Paul was arrested 6 months after we were married. Because he preached the Gospel with such boldness, many people got saved and the communist police wanted to stop him. However, Pastor Paul would not be distracted!

Many times Paul was in and out of prisons, forced labor camps, and re-education camps. He has been in jail so many times that it's hard to keep count! Although it was a slow start, the church grew to 500 members. I taught children Sunday school and led women's ministries, and many women were raised up for the ministry.

We were at this church for 9 years when our fourth child was 8 months old. The police, along with the leaders of that denomination told us to leave the church because Paul had been teaching about the Holy Spirit baptism. Many people had been filled with the Holy Spirit and prayed in tongues.

Training women on being a wife: "manager,"
"lover," "beautiful," "teacher," "helper"

There were 500 people in that church, and we had started 4 other churches, each with 200 members. Even though we had to leave, the churches continued to grow, and even now those 5 churches are still strong in the Lord.Paul and I started underground churches and established cell groups.God used Paul to be the founder of the Assemblies of God in Vietnam. Together we traveled house to house, village to village, and city to city, planting churches – now standing at 266 churches in Vietnam.

Ruth (center) dressed in the tribal costume of one of the minority people groups to which she ministered

I went to the tribes in the mountains and in the countryside to train soul winners, church planters, and preachers. I also trained many women as we started women's ministries.

Later on, women became very important in church planting. The police always paid close attention to the men, but not the women. In many places where the men could not get in, our women were able to go in with the Good News of Jesus Christ and bring change to those places and contribute to the growing church.My husband had been imprisoned because of the Gospel of Jesus Christ.Because he had been arrested several times, he could not return to Vietnam. Therefore, we had to discuss what must be done to get the Gospel to the people. My husband said, "Ruth, you must go and make disciples and teach them about Jesus." So that is what I am doing.

In *Acts 1*, the Holy Spirit came down upon all who were in the upper room, both men and women. In *Romans 2:11*, God says he is not a respecter of persons which means that He does not regard one person more important than another. He empowers male and female. So I, as a woman,have been empowered and have been given authority by the Holy Spirit to preach the Gospel.My husband has given me permission and authority also when he said I must go and make disciples.My husband has sent me as his messenger to be the messenger of the Gospel of our Lord and Savior Jesus Christ.

One time when I was in Vietnam, I had to go to several villages, and transportation was very expensive. Sometimes you are able to take a bus or ride on a moped or bicycle to where you need to go; at other times, you may have to walk. One time, in particular that I remember, we missed the bus ride to the next village, so I had to pay for a moped ride to the next village.

I stayed the night with pig farmers, and it was very cold. The pig pen was very close to the part of the house where I had to sleep, which made it very stinky. The next morning I woke up with a bad pain in my right hip and leg. I was supposed to go that day to teach more people in the next village.

Satan told me I couldn't go because I was in too much pain. I said, "I will go whether I have pain or not." We missed the bus and the next village was several miles away. We had to walk, and then God sent a man with a scooter. Thankfully, he did not overcharge me, so when I got to where I needed to go, I gave him more money than he had asked me to pay. This was a way that I could bless him, and I shared that with him.

My leg and hip were still hurting, but I decided to go on to the next house. When I went into the home of one family, they had a picture of an angel on their wall that drew my attention. The parents told me about their son that was getting sick. The Holy Spirit spoke to me and said that there was a curse on that picture and it must be burned before the family could be blessed.

I told the father, "I cannot burn the picture for you. You must do it for yourself and for your family."He burned the picture and immediately his son became well, and the father accepted Jesus. Their household became blessed. As a matter of fact, they were so blessed that they were able to build a bigger house.So, I went into Vietnam to make disciples and teach about Jesus. The favor of God and the blessing of God were mightily with me. Many came to Christ and became disciples.

If God can use me, he can also use you. There is no more time for excuses.You must choose to go and make disciples for the Lord, for His Kingdom. God will use you even as He has used me! – **Ruth Ai**

Paul and Ruth

Paul and Ruth - on their Wedding Day

Paul and Ruth – Exchanging rings on their Wedding Day

Proverbs 18:22 says, *"He who finds a wife finds what is good and receives favor from the Lord."* God's favor was poured out in my life when He brought Ruth and me together. We have not only been a blessing to each other, but together we have also been able to reach more souls for God's kingdom.

As a team, we have led thousands of people to Christ, have planted several hundred churches, and have discipled and trained hundreds of people.

Paul and Ruth as they were in then -- June 1980

Paul and Ruth as they are today – November 2014

GROWTH OF
THE CHURCH IN VIETNAM| 11

When I was in Bible school in the early seventies, many people asked why I quit Buddhism and witchcraft to follow Jesus. I started sharing my testimony, telling them the story of how people got saved and how I started planting churches in the refugee camp in Long Thanh.

Later, this church went on to become the largest church in Vietnam with over ten thousand believers. It grew because of the signs and wonders that took place and the healings and deliverances that happened. Many people, including young people, were filled with the Holy Spirit.

This first church was in the midst of a very strong Buddhist and Catholic area. In fact, most of the areas where we planted churches were very strong in Buddhism and Catholicism. There were hundreds of Catholic churches in the south because of the immigrants coming from the north in 1954 when the country divided in half due to communism.

We had to use our knowledge and experiences with Buddhism and Catholicism to plant churches in these areas. However, we relied on the power of the Holy Spirit to sow the seeds.

THE MOVE OF GOD AMONG CATHOLICS

As I mentioned earlier, when I was in Bible school I met some Catholic priests and nuns who came to the school to listen to Dr. John Hurston teach about the Holy Spirit baptism and the gifts of the Spirit. They were filled with the Holy Spirit, and God started using them mightily in Vietnam in the late seventies.

Even though all of the evangelical missionaries and Assembly of God pastors had left Vietnam, or were in jail for preaching the Gospel, the Catholics still had freedom. It was during this time that the outpouring of the Holy Spirit occurred through the Catholic charismatic group, and led the way for thousands of Catholics to meet God, become believers, and be filled with the Holy Spirit.

Father Tieu and Father Loc, two of the Catholic priests who had attended Bible college, started a prayer center called Maranatha Center and a program called "*A Ten Day Encounter with the Holy Spirit*". People who participated in the Encounter received daily teaching about God the Father, God the Son, and God the Holy Spirit. The priests taught in detail about the Holy Spirit, including who He is, the fruit of the Holy Spirit, and the gifts of the Holy Spirit. Usually by the sixth or seventh day, people received the infilling of the Holy Spirit and the training continued to teach people how to function in the gifts of the Holy Spirit.

The Catholics were also able to distribute thousands of Bibles that had been left behind by the Gideons and the United Bible Association when they evacuated Vietnam. The evangelicals were not able to easily distribute the Bibles under the new communist government, but the Catholics had the freedom to do so.

GROWTH OF CELL GROUPS

After my escape from prison in 1979, I continued preaching and training with boldness. I believed God and that nothing was impossible for Him, and I knew that it was only through the power of the Holy Spirit that I was able to be successful, *"'Not by might, nor by power, but by my Spirit,' says the Lord."*– Zechariah 4:6b

At this time God began to teach me more about cell groups. The New Testament describes them as meeting in homes in *Romans 16:5*; *Acts 20:18-20*; *Colossians 4:15*; and *Philemon 2*. In fact, whenever two or three gather, Jesus said that He will be in the midst of them (see *Matthew 18:20*).

I learned that the church in China and in Muslim countries grows through cell groups meeting in homes. Even in countries with religious freedom, such as South Korea, cell groups were key factors that contributed to making Dr. Yonggi Cho's church the largest in the world.

When people accepted Jesus as their Savior, I took time to disciple them. I trained them on how to win souls through sharing their testimony and the good news of Jesus. After they concluded this training, I continued to train them on how to lead a cell group and then on how to start a new church.

First Bible school; each person is now a leader
of a denomination in Vietnam

With this approach, the Lord blessed our church and it grew to 500 members. The first church was started in Trang-Bom and from this church we planted six other churches in Kinh-Te-Moi, Dau-Day, Bau-Ca, Cay-Gao, Tri-An, and Ho Nai.

Because of my continued boldnes to preach, teach and start churches, I was arrested many times in 1980 – 1985. My sentence for prison each time ranged from a couple days to a couple months. No matter how long they kept me in prison though, the church kept growing. Soul winners, cell leaders, and church planters worked with the Holy Spirit to increase the church.

The rapid growth of the church not only attracted the attention of the police, but also drew the attention of Christians in different areas of Vietnam. Christians from other churches were challenged to look at how the church was growing so quickly.

Over the next year, many came to learn how we were training people and sending them out. They returned to their areas and became witnesses for the Lord. Some were successful and some were not. Some churches sent their people out, but did not succeed; so they asked me to conduct some training.

TRAINING PASTORS

From 1985 to 1988, I held many seminars and classes to train soul winners, cell leaders, and church planters. I emphasized the Baptism of the Holy Spirit, which is the power and the key to winning souls and planting churches. In Luke 24:49 Jesus commanded His disciples to wait in Jerusalem until they received power from above.

In Mark 16, Jesus promised that whoever believed would receive the gift of the Holy Spirit. In Acts 1:4-8, Jesus promised that He would baptize them with the power of the Holy Spirit and when they received that power, they would become His witnesses in Jerusalem, Judea, Samaria, and to the ends of the world.

I explained to people, "If you are not successful in your 'Jerusalem,' your community, how can you be successful elsewhere? The only thing that will cause you to be successful is to be filled with the Holy Spirit."

After that, people began seeking the Baptism in the Holy Spirit. Many of them experienced being filled with the Holy Spirit and power, and they preached the Gospel with anointing. The church grew incredibly and the government was upset. They decided to stop me, and with the help of the pro-government churches, they did.

They decided to deport me from the church where I had spent the last five years training people, discipling people, and planting churches. Through the power of the Holy Spirit and through the discipleship program, seven churches had been planted. Now, the government gave me 48 hours to pack up my family and leave permanently.

Baptismal service in the ceramic factory

Since pastors of churches in Vietnam live at the church with their family, this church had been our home for five years. Now, we had no place to live and no means of support.I started working in the marketing department for a ceramic company that was on the verge of closing. I made two deals with them: 1) Ten percent of their profits would go to missions to preach the Gospel. 2) They would let me use their facility for meetings and baptism.

In return, I would help them market their product and build their company into a successful business. Each day, after I worked in the office, I went out to sell the product. I would then spend time sharing Christ with the customers. "He's the One who changed my life and He's much better than the product that I showed you."

People began to get saved and filled with the Holy Spirit. Two months later, I had a new church. I spent most of my time training and equipping the new believers. They began sharing with their friends, and the church started growing.

METHODS OF DISCIPLESHIP | 12

During my first term in prison, God reminded me of the Great Commission in *Matthew 28:18-20*. God told me, "When you get out of prison, go to disciple all nations."

In **Mark 16:16-20**, Jesus prophesied, *"Whoever believes and is baptized will be saved, but whoever does not believe will be condemned. And these signs will accompany those who believe: In my name they will drive out demons; they will speak in new tongues; ...they will place their hands on sick people and they will get well. Then the disciples went out and preached everywhere and the Lord worked with them and confirmed His word by the signs that accompanied it."*

The Great Commission is this: every believer has to go out to preach the Gospel and as we go out, God will give His signs, wonders, and miracles to accompany and to confirm His word. God spoke to me that this new church would be an apostolic church, operating in signs, wonders and miracles. This message was the basis for training people and sending them out to preach the Gospel. If they would do their job, God would do His. From this sprang the strategy for discipleship training and church planting.

AVOIDING DETECTION

Of course reaching and teaching others for Christ is illegal in Vietnam. It is not illegal to be a Christian, but it is illegal to evangelize and disciple people outside of the covering of the communist government. If a church is not registered with the government, then the church members cannot meet together.

However, in order to be registered with the government, a church cannot actively evangelize and cannot preach about the Second Coming of Jesus, among other things. Everyone who wants to be baptized in the government-sanctioned church has to submit a resume and register to be baptized.

Training in a rice field

In order not to be detected by the police, we had to be creative in the locations we trained people. For example, we rented a tour bus, but instead of telling people about the sites, I taught them about the Bible. If we were stopped by the police, then we would turn on the tour video and everyone pretended to be tourists.

We rented boats to take a short cruise. We would anchor a ways off shore and conduct training. It was easy to see the police coming, so people would get in the water to swim, and it seemed that we were just having a party.

Using a tour bus as a training facility

We also used hotel rooms, rice fields, the jungle, and ironically even government facility classrooms.Students in the training classes had to take their notes on very small pieces of paper. Their homework assignment was to re-copy their notes into their notebook when they got home.

This way, even if they were stopped by the police for questioning on their way home, they could eat the small pieces of paper so that there would be no evidence that they were involved in Christian discipleship training.

TRAINING OTHERS TO FOLLOW CHRIST

Early in my ministry the Holy Spirit guided me to create a structured approach to discipling new Christians and to train believers to be soul winners, cell leaders, church planters, pastors and ordained ministers. Each of these levels of training covered topics relevant to being a Christian, leading others to follow Christ and then leading and starting new churches.

It provided a good foundation for living a Christian life and acted as a filter for communist infiltrators into church leadership. The basic training for new converts laid the foundation for understanding their salvation and the basic doctrines of the Bible.

The Vietnamese people have a background of worshiping many different gods. They have to realize that Jesus is not another god that they can add to their list. I wrote lessons to teach them to renounce all their other gods and to accept Jesus Christ as the only God and Savior of their life.

Topics include:

1) *Prayer – what to pray and how to pray*
2) *God – who God is*
3) *Man – who man is and where he came from*
4) *Sin – what it is and the results of sin*
5) *Salvation – what it means*
6) *Savior – about Jesus*
7) *Worship – what it is and how to worship*
8) *Church ordinances – baptism and communion*
9) *Evangelism – what it is and how to do it*
10) *Giving tithes and offerings*

Worshipping at a disco club during the day so that we can be loud and not be heard

Forevery lesson there are also about ten questions on that lesson's topic. At the end of these three months, the new converts take a test. If they score over seventy percent, then we spend time interviewing them for water baptism.

After water baptism, they start with the first level of training called "Caleb" or "Soul Winner." Caleb was the one who brought God's people Israel out of Egypt, darkness, into Canaan, light. So, the idea of this level is that Caleb is a soul winner to bring people out of spiritual darkness into light.

After one month of training on how to be a soul winner, we send them out and give them one month to practice by winning five souls to the Lord and reading through the Bible one time. If they meet these requirements, we arrange for them to come back for the second level of training.

We call the second level "Joshua." In the Joshua level we train people to be cell leaders. Joshua was the man who brought God's people into the Promised Land and our

Promised Land today is the Baptism of the Holy Spirit, together with the gifts and fruit of the Holy Spirit.

Meeting in the jungle for training

In the Joshua level, we train for three months in eighteen courses.

We cover the following topics:

1) *Becoming a Witness to People*
2) *Leading People to Accept Jesus as Lord and Savior*
3) *Following Up with New Converts*
4) *Counseling New Converts*
5) *Starting a Cell Group*
6) *Leading your Cell Group in Bible Study*
7) *Leading Worship in Your Cell Group*
8) *Leading People to Receive the Holy Spirit's Baptism*
9) *Becoming Soul Winners*
10) *Operating in the Gifts of the Holy Spirit*
11) *Praying for the Sick*
12) *Praying for Deliverance*
13) *Praying Successfully*
14) *Knowing God's Will*
15) *Preparing a Sermon*
16) *Leading God's Servants*

After three months of training at the Joshua level, we send them back to their villages and give them three months to practice. They have to win another fifteen souls and read the Bible four more times.

We call the third level, "Andrew," the church planter level. Andrew was the man who Jesus asked to feed the flock. Therefore, in the "Andrew" level we train people to become a church planter through eighteen courses.

They are challenged to teach their church to tithe and give offerings, have at least twenty members who have been baptized in water and in the Holy Spirit, and meet together every Sunday. After they meet these requirements, they are licensed to go to the fourth level.

Training on a boat

The fourth level is called, "Aaron," or the local pastor level. At the level of a local pastor, they are required to plant a local, self-supporting church before being licensed as a minister and training others. Meeting these requirements will allow the person to move on to level five.

Level five is called, "Moses." At this level, the person will become an ordained minister if he or she meets all of the requirements. The candidate at this level must study for a Bachelor's degree equivalent to 128 credits. Their church must have planted a new church within two years, or they must have been arrested and imprisoned for preaching the Gospel. While in prison they should have planted a new church.

These five levels are the strategy God gave me for raising up leaders and growing the church in Vietnam. This strategy is also a way that God protects the church from being destroyed from the inside-out in Vietnam. The police often infiltrate the church with undercover agents as spies to identify people who are the leaders in the church. Their goal is to learn all they can about who is involved, especially in leadership, and what activities are being planned.

When these undercover agents come in, they can go through all the motions of accepting the Lord as their Savior, from going throughdiscipleship course andto getting baptized. Some of

Baptizing between two boats to avoid detection

them can even make it through the "Caleb" level. That is where it stops, however. The next level, the "Joshua" level, requires demonstration of the power of the Holy Spirit. Since they are not able to fake or copy the power of the Holy Spirit when they are faced with praying for healing or deliverance, they cannot progress through this level, nor move on to the "Andrew" level.

God began by saving and delivering me from the darkness of Buddhism and witchcraft. He then trained me to lead His people and gave me the strategy to use women in ministry.

The model He gave me for discipleship was designed for the protection and growth of His Church in Vietnam. Through the outpouring of His Spirit, and the obedience and faithfulness of His people, the church has grown and continues to be strong in the Lord and in His mighty power.

The first Sunday after the fall of Saigon was not only a turning point in my life, but it was also a turning point in the strategy that God showed me for ministry. As I looked out on my congregation that Sunday morning, I realized that only the women had shown up for church service. At that moment God began to give me a plan for women to do the work of ministry.

The idea of women in ministry was a challenge for me. In Vietnamese culture women are not well respected and they are not regarded as equal to men. For example, it is a custom for women to walk three steps behind their husband. God had to change my cultural perspective through His Word.

As I searched the Bible, I found out that Peter reminded the Jews in Jerusalem on the day of Pentecost that the prophet Joel said:

"And it shall come to pass in the last days, saith God, I will pour out of my Spirit upon all flesh: and your sons and your daughters shall prophesy, and your young men shall see visions, and your old men shall dream dreams: And on my servants and on my handmaidens I will pour out in those days of my Spirit; and they shall prophesy:"
(Acts 2:16-18, KJV)

In *Galatians 3:28*, the Apostle Paul wrote that in God there is "neither male nor female." I also found out that in communist countries such as China and even developed countries such as South Korea, God was using many women in the ministry. So, I continued studying the Bible to really make sure I was gaining the right understanding.

Women praying from the high places over the village
before going to evangelize

I found an example of fearless female leadership in *Exodus 1:15-21*. Two of the midwives of the Hebrew people, Shiphrah and Puah feared God rather than the king or the government at that time by refusing to obey the decree to kill the Hebrew baby boys as they were born. These two women were bold and had the fear of God rather than the fear of man. They risked their own lives to protect God's people and do God's will.

Another example of fearless female leadership is the story of Rahab. In *Joshua chapters 2 and 6, Hebrews 11:31, and James 2:25*, we read how Rahab, who had been a prostitute, was used by God to rescue the Hebrew spies. She had faith in God and feared God more than the king. I have seen in my own life that when people truly fear God, then they are not afraid of anything else.

I continued to read the Bible and found that in *Judges, chapters 4 and 5*, Deborah showed courage in the day of trouble, as she stood strong and won the battle. Anna, in *Luke 2*, is another example of a faithful intercessor that is willing to stand in the gap through prayer.Another great example is Mary, the mother of Jesus. In *Luke 1:45-49*, she shows boldness and faith in God and in what He said that He is going to do through her and for their people. Later on, we see her at the wedding in Cana telling others to listen to Jesus and to do what He tells them *(John 2)*.

She also followed Jesus listening to His teaching. She was at Calvary when Jesus was crucified. In the Book of Acts, she and many other women were faithful in fasting and praying until the time that they were filled with the Holy Spirit on the day of Pentecost.*Mark 16* mentions several women who were at the crucifixion of Jesus and remained faithful to Him even when it was difficult and uncertain times.

Many of the men had left Jesus. The women were willing to take a risk. They were not afraid of the Roman government or of the Jewish religious leaders. They went all the way to the grave to minister to Jesus with spices for His body.

When they saw that He was not there and were told by the angels that Jesus had risen, they boldly went and spread the good news to the other disciples without regard for how they would be perceived. Even though most of the disciples doubted what they were saying, the women continued to preach the good news.

I found out that in the time of darkness, in the time of trouble, the women are not only faithful in the quiet place to pray and intercede; they will show up and take a risk to accomplish the task. That is why I am encouraged and have the boldness to trust the Word of God to train and equip women to do ministry.

When I was the General Superintendent of the Assemblies of God in Vietnam, we had over 200 churches in our fellowship, and two-thirds of them were being led by women. The Assemblies of God of Vietnam was the first denomination in Vietnam that ordained, licensed, or certified women to lead underground churches in Vietnam.

Whenever we would come together for district council meetings, people would tell me, "Oh, Pastor Ai, thank you for giving us a woman pastor. Since the woman pastor has come to our church, the church has really grown." "What do you mean?" I asked them. "Well, women like to tell stories and since you trained them to tell good stories, they are able to tell stories about Jesus and people want to accept Him as their Savior. So many people

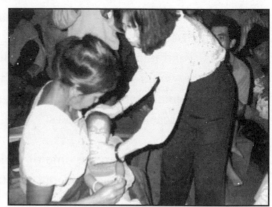

Ruth praying - a baby who was brought back to life

have come to church and how the church has grown."

Another person told me, "Since you gave us a woman pastor, our church has really become prosperous. Women are not afraid to talk about tithing and giving. They explain how God will bless us when we give, and they will not stop until everyone has given!"

Over and over again I heard and saw evidence that God was blessing women in ministry. One such woman was Thuy. She was a very tough woman from Northern Vietnam when she first came to our church.

She accepted the Lord as her Savior, and we prayed for her. God directed her to quit her job and go to Bible school. After she graduated, she boldly went to preach the Gospel and start a church. Soon, she was arrested and put in jail. We hired a lawyer to fight for her, but he lost the case. (However, he accepted Jesus as his Lord and Savior as a result of her testimony. Later, this lawyer brought two other lawyers to know the Lord and they started a Christian law office that stood against persecution.)

During Pastor Thuy's time in jail, she led many people to the Lord. Her story also became well-known to many Christian organizations around the world which petitioned the Vietnamese government for her release. When she was released from prison, she went back to her town and continued to minister.

God blessed the ministry and many people's lives were changed. She built a church building, and the church quickly grew in number of people and was blessed in finances, so they were able to build a bigger building. Pastor Thuy became well-known for her ministry and the persecution that she had endured. God continued to bless her and many lives have been impacted by her ministry.

In the beginning of Thuy's ministry, my wife went to visit her. She remembers having to sleep next to the pig pen because they were so poor they had no other place for her to sleep.

After Thuy showed herself faithful to God and bold to preach His Word, not only did the church grow and was financially blessed, but now she was personally blessed with a nice house.

Another woman from the Central Highlands in Vietnam was very young when she went to Bible school. The Central Highlands of Vietnam has very tight security; yet within ten years after Bible school, she was able to plant 66 churches in the area. Men would not have been able to do this because of the communist security police surveillance. Later on, this woman became the Assemblies of God Superintendent of the Central Highlands District with 66 churches under her leadership.

In Vietnam, many places that men cannot go, women are able to go. There are many villages that I could not visit without drawing a lot of attention and arousing suspicion. Ruth, however, would dress as the people of the village and was able to easily go into the village undetected and then minister to people. She would start a church, and then later on, I was able to go visit.

The Bible makes very clear that God pours out His Spirit on women, as well as men. In Christ, there is no more male or female. (Galatians 3:28) The fact is that throughout the Bible, we see how God raised up women to do His will.

We also see in modern history how God has raised up women to bring the Gospel into areas that men cannot go, and to lead his Body in times that men cannot lead.

I continue to encourage women not to be shy or quiet, but to be bold because God will use you just as He uses men. In fact, in the day of trouble, if the men disappear, God will put in your heart courage, boldness and faithfulness.

So, women, this is the time for you to stand up, to arise, to shine, because the power of God will come upon you, and you will do a great job, even better than many men in the time of darkness.

REACHING THE ILLITERATE | 14

In the remote countryside villages and the mountainous regions of Vietnam there are many ethnic minorities who have never heard about Christ. Very few of them can read or write, so God gave me a way to reach them with the Gospel message and to disciple them in basic doctrine without requiring them to read or write.

Ruth and I have a passion to see every Vietnamese person hear the Gospel, so when we lived in Vietnam, we

I'm dressed in communist garb and posing as a vendor in order to easily get into the village

would often travel to these remote areas to minister. We had to be creative in how we tried to blend in with the people of the area we were visiting; otherwise, we would easily draw attention to ourselves and raise the suspicion of the security police. We would dress in the ethnic clothing of the areas we were visiting, or if it was a strong communist area, then I would dress as a communist party member.

In our outreaches, Ruth and I shared the Gospel using pictures with which people could relate. The pictures illustrated in this chapter demonstrate the condition of the human heart, our need for salvation, and the results of a life at peace with God.

After one week of training using the pictures, we sent people back to their villages with the pictures to lead people to Christ and even start churches. We continued to disciple them through using pictures, but we also taught them to read and write. Many people trained under us went on to earn college degrees because of the training that we gave them.

Many evil things fill our hearts such as:

- pride (peacock)
- adultery (goat)
- gluttony (pig)
- lust or a desire to attack or kill (wolf)
- lying and deception (snake)
- anger (tiger)
- laziness (turtle)

The Word of God (book) and the Holy Spirit (dove) lead us to salvation of Jesus (cross).

Satan tempts people and brings them to hell.

When you accept Jesus as your Savior, your spiritual eyesare opened. As you study the Word of God and listen to the Holy Spirit, your eyes continue to be opened.

People who drift from the Word of God and the Holy Spirit have their consciences (star) desensitized to the things of God and begin to allow the other things back into their hearts.

For many years, under communism, it was illegal to own a Bible, so there were no Bibles available for purchase in Vietnam. The Bibles that we had were the ones left behind by the Gideons and the United Bible Association when they evacuated Vietnam in the seventies. The only new Bibles we had were the ones that missionaries and other Christians smuggled into the country.

Since there were not enough Bibles, we would handwrite copies of the Bible. Each family was assigned a portion of the Bible to copy. If someone could not read and write when they became a Christian, we taught them, so that they could also copy a portion of the Bible.

I could not have a Bible while I was in prison, so my wife had to come up with creative ways to get pages of the Bible to me. One thing that I was allowed to have in prison was a dictionary, so Ruth would hide single pages torn out of a Bible in the pages of a dictionary.

In 1989 the Assembly of God church denomination was really growing in Vietnam, and I asked pastor Luciano to come help. Pastor Luciano was one of the missionaries who discipled me after I became a Christian. When he started working with us, he saw the great need for Bibles to be published. I gave Luciano a copy of one of the handwritten Bibles, and he used it to raise money to buy 7,000 Bibles.

The Bibles we purchased had to be shipped from Thailand. This was a risky undertaking, as it would be extremely difficult to hide a shipment of 7,000 Bibles from the police. The organization that we were working with on this project wanted the Bibles to be kept in Thailand, and then smuggled a few at a time into Vietnam.

Their plan was to have mission teams going from Thailand to Vietnam to carry the Bibles into Vietnam. The problem with this plan was that the mission teams only came about four times each year, and each person on the team could only carry five Bibles. It would take too long for 7,000 Bibles to be smuggled in to the country.

Luciano and I found a different way to get the Bibles from Thailand through Laos, and then in to Vietnam. We decided simply to ship them on two trucks. Once we had the Bibles in the country, we planned to distribute them slowly and carefully so as not to attract the attention of the police. We stored the Bibles at someone's house and then a few people at a time would visit the house and leave with one or two Bibles.

Some people had never had a Bible, and others had not seen a printed Bible in a long time, so they were eager to get one. One pastor was so excited that he did not follow our instructions to take only one or two Bibles. He took a whole box of Bibles. Before he got home, he was stopped by the police who wanted to know the contents of the box he was carrying.

When they discovered what was in the box, they began to ask questions. This pastor had a large church that was registered with the government, so he did not want to be arrested and put in jail. He would lose everything. He cooperated with the police interrogation and told them where the Bibles were located, and the security police confiscated all the Bibles.

Celebrating the first Bibles being printed in Vietnam under Communism, 1995

Many people, including the organization that had given us the Bibles, were really upset with me and with Luciano. All we could do was pray for God's wisdom for a way to get the Bibles back. We had an idea to ask one of the women in our church to speak to the wife of one of the security officers who had confiscated the Bibles.

After she read some of the Bible to the lady and her husband, she pleaded, "Please do not destroy the Bibles. Instead, sell them to us and you can make money." Miraculously, the authorities allowed us to purchase the Bibles back for five dollars a copy.

The fact that we were able to smuggle in 7,000 Bibles without detection really concerned the Vietnamese government. They thought, "If they smuggled 7,000 Bibles all the way from Thailand, to Laos, to Cambodia, they can do anything else."

This incident pressured the government to allow Bibles to be printed in Vietnam. I was invited to join the celebration of the printing of the first Bibles under communism in Vietnam in 1995.

COMING TO
THE UNITED STATES| 16

When I was arrested in Hanoi in 1999, I was put in the "Hanoi Hilton," the notorious prison of the Vietnam War. It was still a horrendous prison, and I learned that this time the police had plans to kill me. Through God's intervention, however, I became extremely ill and was sent to the hotel across the street from the prison. To the world, it seemed I had been released from prison. In reality, however, I was under confinement to my hotel room while under the care of a doctor.

At the same time this was happening, the U.S. government was petitioning the Vietnam government for my release. I was finally released and allowed to return to Saigon under house arrest until arrangements could be made for me and my family to leave Vietnam. It took several months for the details to be arranged for our sponsorship by a church in the U.S. The basis of our entry into the U.S. was religious asylum.

I still remember the night we received word that we would be allowed to leave Vietnam. It was a beautiful, clear evening in December 1999. We were given only 24 hours to pack what we could and prepare to leave our home. We were looking forward to a new life in the U.S., but we were very sad to leave behind all that we knew in Vietnam.

We had many invitations from churches all over the U.S. to be a part of their church family, but God told me that we were to go to Bethel Temple in Hampton, VA. People from our new church family greeted us at the airport and brought us to our new home. Someone had given us a house, and people from the church furnished it with everything we needed. It was Christmastime, and they had even decorated for Christmas and had gifts for all of us!

On the way to our new home from the airport, my son asked if I was going to be put in prison anymore for preaching the Gospel. He was relieved when he learned that we would have freedom here to worship God and to preach the Gospel.Now, my children would not be restrained from receiving a good education because their father was a minister. Now, I did not have to sleep with my backpack next to me in case I was arrested. Now, my wife would not have to wonder whether I would be home that night, or in prison. It was a relief and a blessing to be in the United States.

MINISTRY TO VIETNAM WAR VETERANS

Since I have come to the U.S., I have not only the freedom to preach and teach the Gospel, I also have the opportunity to reach out to many Vietnam War veterans and their families to thank them for the many good things they did for Vietnam.

Because the men and women in uniform went to Vietnam with M16 rifles, they opened the door for missionaries to come to Vietnam with "John 3:16 Bibles." Sadly, however, after they came back to the U.S. many veterans faced problems in their lives with their families, their friends, and mental and physical distress which has continued through the years.

Some of this is a result of the curses that were put on them while they were in Vietnam. Many of the veterans that have received physical and mental support since they have returned still suffer because of the spiritual effects of the curses.

I have had the opportunity to pray with a lot of veterans and encourage them. Many veterans who have been to our meetings have been set free from their torment. God has used me to bring reconciliation, healing, deliverance, and hope for their future.

I tell them that the devil came to steal, to kill, to destroy and mess up their lives; but Jesus came to rescue them, set them free, bless them and give them a bright future. This is one of the purposes for which God has brought us to the U.S., and I thank Him for using me to bring freedom and hope to the Vietnam veterans.

ENCOURAGEMENT TO AND PARTNERSHIP WITH THE CHURCH

Another purpose for God bringing us to the U.S. is to travel to encourage people about missions. I am the fruit of people who supported missions. I thank God for the churches which prayed, gave, and sent people like Pastor Carrie Hunsburger, Pastor Lester Keeney, Reverend Henry Swain, and Reverend Irvin Rutherford to missions. They were sent to Vietnam to help equip our church. According to *Philippians 4*, God will give a great financial harvest when people invest into missions.

I also thank God that since we came to the U.S., we have many believers and churches partnering with us to send us out to reach the Vietnamese working around the world. Many Vietnamese are sent out as contract workers to other countries to bring money back to Vietnam. When these young people were in Vietnam they were not allowed to hear the Gospel, and of course we were not allowed to preach the Gospel to them.

Now that they are in countries such as Cambodia, Laos, Malaysia, Korea, and Kuwait, we are able to reach them with the Gospel. When we speak to them, we find that they are so hungry to hear about Jesus. In the past eight years, one thousand contract workers from Vietnam have been brought into God's Kingdom.

One hundred churches have been started in these areas, and hundreds of churches have been started in Vietnam when these workers return to their villages and share the Gospel with their families and friends. So, I thank all of our partners for joining us in the opportunity to reach out to the Vietnamese around the world to enlarge God's Kingdom.

In 2000, soon after we arrived in the U.S., I was invited by the church in England to address the Parliament and the Queen regarding religious freedom in Vietnam. I was also invited by Dr. Billy Graham to join him in a crusade in Amsterdam, Holland. I was honored to receive these invitations, but unfortunately if I left the United States for any reason, my visa would have expired and I would be banned from the United States too!

We immediately began planning how we could minister to the Vietnamese living in the U.S. There are more than two million Vietnamese who live outside of Vietnam, the majority of whom reside in the U.S. We founded Vietnamese Outreach International to be able to reach, touch, train, and send Vietnamese with the Gospel around the world.

We immediately started a Vietnamese congregation at Bethel Temple in Hampton, and then as God began to open up opportunities to travel and preach around the world, we had to relinquish being pastors of one church. We now focus on reaching the thousands of Vietnamese migrant workers around the world with the Gospel. We have started churches in Korea, Laos, Cambodia, Malaysia, and even in Kuwait.

We concentrate most of our ministry training in Southeast Asia. Our vision is to train and disciple Vietnamese believers to reach their families, friends and communities for Christ when they return to Vietnam.

RETURN TO VIETNAM

In February 2009, Ruth and I received our U.S. citizenship. It is a blessing to have a U.S. passport. Unless you have traveled with a passport from another country, it is difficult to understand what it really means to have a U.S. passport. Customs officials treat us with more respect than when we had our Vietnamese passports.

Since God has called me to reach Vietnam for Him, I have tried several times to get back into Vietnam after we left in 1999, but it was to no avail. Each time, I was detained at the airport, interrogated, and then deported to Singapore. My name is on the list of people not permitted into Vietnam.

There were only two times before I received my U.S. passport that I was able to get in to Vietnam. The first time, I obtained a visa through a travel agency in Cambodia. The consulate in the area did not have direct access to the database of dissidents not allowed into Vietnam, so I was issued a visa.

I boarded a boat and took a route that I had not used before, so the police would not recognize me. I was able to get through security, but it was only one day before the police learned I was there. They followed me everywhere I went, and eventually forced me to leave.

The second time I was able to go in to Vietnam was when my mother-in-law died. I had a travel document that had my name as *Ai Tran*, instead of *Tran Dinh Ai*. By changing my name around, I was not easily recognized at the border. I went to her funeral, spent three days with my family, and then I had to leave.

When I received my U.S. citizenship, I thought, "Praise God! Now, my name is different and I am a U.S. citizen. I will not have any trouble getting a visa to visit Vietnam." Shortly after Ruth and I received our new passports, we applied for a visa to Vietnam. Sure enough, I had no trouble getting the visa, and I had no trouble getting through customs at the border.

A pastor from the U.S. joined me and we started doing some pastoral training with about eighty church leaders. The second day, the group nearly doubled in size. I knew that word was quickly spreading about me being in Vietnam. People wanted to come see me and to hear our teaching.

I told the other pastor, "We cannot stay here and continue our teaching. We must leave now. The police know that I am here, and they will be looking for me." So, we left to visit my family in the country.

While I was visiting my family, I noticed that the police started following me wherever I went. The pastor and I returned to the city, and then he left Vietnam. I stayed, however, because I wanted to learn what was happening. The police followed me to my hotel and booked a room right next to mine. Every time I left the hotel, they followed me. They even sat next to me at restaurants. I could not get away from them.

Very soon, I received an "invitation" from them to come to the security police station to talk with them. Now, an "invitation" from the security police is more like a summons to appear. If you do not, then they will find you and bring you to meet with them.So I went to police station and they began to interrogate me.

They also illegally confiscated my passport. I informed them that they were not allowed to take my passport and they should return it to me. They returned it to me, but instructed that I was not allowed to leave the hotel where I was staying. They would be watching me. I was further instructed to return to the police station the next day for further discussion.

When I returned to my hotel, I contacted the U.S. Embassy, and also called back to the U.S. to contact my senator's office. The following day, a representative from the embassy escorted me to the police station and informed them that they could not detain me. They agreed to leave me alone, if I agreed to leave Vietnam. The consular advised me to do so, or he could do nothing further to help me.

During this ordeal, I learned just how much of an impact I and Ruth have had in Vietnam since we have been reaching and teaching Vietnamese migrant workers with the Gospel. The police informed me that hundreds of churches have been started in the mountain regions of Vietnam, and, "We know you have something to do with this! We know that you are teaching people outside of Vietnam and sending them back. These people are radical."

It is funny to me that I was able to learn about the scope of the spread of the Gospel from the very people who are trying to stop me! God has a sense of humor.

Ruth and I continue to reach souls for Jesus. God has appointed us to reach Vietnam with the Gospel. We want all Vietnamese to be able to hear the message of salvation through Jesus Christ!

VISION OF VIETNAMESE OUTREACH INTERNATIONAL

The mission of VOI is to bring people out of the kingdom of darkness into the kingdom of light, out of the kingdom of Satan into the kingdom of God, as described in *Acts 26:16-20*. Our vision is to see believers expand the Kingdom of God through soul winning, multiplying disciples, and equipping others to do the work of the ministry as cell leaders, church planters, and pastors.

OUR CURRENT STRATEGY

Equip Saints for Work of Ministry in Southeast Asia

In the Bible, there are three categories of gifts: 1) Gifts of Service in *Romans 12*; 2) Gifts of the manifestation of the power of God through the Holy Spirit in *I Corinthians 12; and 3*) Gifts of equipping the saints for the work of ministry in *Ephesians 4*.

God is a God of teamwork. God the Father, the Son, and the Holy Spirit worked together in Creation, in Salvation, and in Benediction. So, God intends for teamwork. I believe that the church needs to train and equip people to work as a team.

Since I cannot go into Vietnam, yet, I still train in Southeast Asia. We started a training center in Cambodia. We thank God that Vision International University recognized our work and approved *Vision International Harvest College.* Vietnamese pastors from Laos, Cambodia and Vietnam can attend VIHC to be equipped to do ministry. We will increase the training sessions to every three months to bring pastors from all over SE Asia to train them to grow the church and to grow in their knowledge of the Word and how to do ministry.

When pastors complete the program, they will receive their diploma and have the opportunity to work toward their Bachelor and Master's degrees. We are praying that God will touch people to partner with us in financial support to sponsor pastors who desire to obtain their Bachelor's and Master's degrees.

There are many costs incurred as the pastors have to travel from their towns to Cambodia. Transportation, lodging, and food costs can be too much for pastors who make only enough money to care for their families.We want to train and equip every believer to become a soul winner and a cell leader, church planter and church leader who can survive and thrive under persecution!

Plant churches in Vietnam

As more soul winners and cell leaders are raised up, they become church planters. It is a three to five year structured process to become a church planter. We need people to partner with us in supporting church planters in large cities, small towns, and in rural villages. The costs to support a church planter vary depending on the location of the church planted.

Rescue children from prostitution and forced labor in Cambodia

God has also led us to reach out to Vietnamese orphans in Cambodia. We were faced with this reality when we discovered that many children are sold into prostitution to provide money for their families. We started Children's Lighthouse Refuge to feed, clothe, educate, and disciple them so that they will not be sold into prostitution or forced into hard labor. Our vision is to not only train and equip them to be soul winners, cell leaders and church planters, but to also rescue other children out of prostitution and poverty by starting other *Lighthouses* throughout Cambodia and eventually Vietnam.

FRUIT OF OUR LABOR

We wish to convey our sincerest *"Thank You"* to the people who believe in winning souls and training them to be soul winners, cell leaders, and church planters. Because of the partnership of believers and churches, Ruth and I are able to go to Laos, Cambodia, Korea, and Kuwait to bring Good News to the Vietnamese workers. Not only do we lead them to the Lord, but we are also able to spend time to train them to be strong and to survive when they go back to Vietnam.

The government will use their families to persecute them. Many of them come from a background of communism, Buddhism, atheism, or ancestor worship, so they will be persecuted now that they worship Jesus. We train them on how to share the Gospel through sharing their testimony of how God has blessed them. We train them how to win souls, so that they can lead their families and neighbors to the Lord.

We train them how to be a cell leader so that they understand how to lead a cell group in their home. We also train them how to grow the cell group into becoming a church so they can be a church planter. Next, they become a local pastor. After that, if they show potential, we train them to become a church leader so they can plant other churches out of their church and become the leadership in that area.

WE THANK GOD FOR YOUR PRAYERS
AND PARTNERSHIP!

VALUABLE LESSONS | 18

SUBMITTING TO AUTHORITY WHEN AUTHORITY IS OPPOSED TO GOD

"What if tomorrow you were placed in handcuffs for preaching the Gospel?" This is one of the first questions I ask my Bible school students and it is one of the first teachings they receive before they start their classes.

Two of the most common questions I am asked as I travel and share my testimony are, "How do you submit to authorities when they go against what God tells you?" and, "How can you overcome all the suffering and persecution you face as a result of doing what God wants?" The short answer is, "If you renew your mind with His Word, then you will have the courage to face persecution and overcome it."

OBEY THE HIGHEST AUTHORITY

The Bible tells us that we are to submit ourselves to the authorities over us. Since God is the highest authority, then we must choose to obey Him when all other authorities in our lives are telling us to do something contrary to what He has said.

This is made clear in Scripture:

Everyone must submit himself to the governing authorities, for there is no authority except that which God has established.The authorities that exist have been established by God. Consequently, he who rebels against the authority is rebelling against what God has instituted, and those who do so will bring judgment on themselves. For rulers hold no terror for those who do right, but for those who do wrong. Do you want to be free from fear of the one in authority? Then do what is right and he will commend you. For he is God's servant to do you good. But if you do wrong, be afraid, for he does not bear the sword for nothing. He is God's servant, an agent of wrath to bring punishment on the wrongdoer. Therefore, it is necessary to submit to the authorities, not only because of possible punishment but also because of conscience.
(Romans 13:1-5)

But Peter and John replied, "Judge for yourselves whether it is right in God's sight to obey you rather than God."
(Acts 4:19)

Peter and the other apostles replied: "We must obey God rather than men!"
(Acts 5:29)

BUILD YOURSELF UP

Learn what God says about persecution, and encourage yourself with the promises of His Word. God gives us power so we can be strong:

For God did not give us a spirit of timidity, but a spirit of power, of love and of self-discipline. So do not be ashamed to testify about our Lord, or ashamed of me his prisoner. But join with me in suffering for the gospel, by the power of God.(II Timothy 1:7-8)

Just as Paul, we do not have to be ashamed to testify, to be put in prison, or to suffer for the Lord Jesus:

Coming over to us, he took Paul's belt, tied his own hands and feet with it and said, "The Holy Spirit says, 'In this way the Jews of Jerusalem will bind the owner of this belt and will hand him over to the Gentiles.'" When we heard this, we and the people there pleaded with Paul not to go up to Jerusalem. Then Paul answered, "Why are you weeping and breaking my heart? I am ready not only to be bound, but also to die in Jerusalem for the name of the Lord Jesus." When he would not be dissuaded, we gave up and said, "The Lord's will be done." After this, we got ready and went up to Jerusalem.(Acts 21:11-15)

Believe that in all things God works things out for good to those love Him:

And we know that in all things God works for the good of those who love him, who have been called according to his purpose. (Romans 8:28)

Give thanks to God in all circumstances:

Give thanks in all circumstances, for this is God's will for you in Christ Jesus. (I Thessalonians 5:18)

We do not need to fear man:

What you have said in the dark will be heard in the daylight, and what you have whispered in the ear in the inner rooms will be proclaimed from the roofs."I tell you, my friends, do not be afraid of those who kill the body and after that can do no more. But I will show you whom you should fear: Fear him who, after the killing of the body, has power to throw you into hell. Yes, I tell you, fear him. Are not five sparrows sold for two pennies? Yet not one of them is forgotten by God. Indeed, the very hairs of your head are all numbered. Don't be afraid; you are worth more than many sparrows.(Luke 12:3-7)

God will be with us:

But before all this, they will lay hands on you and persecute you. They will deliver you to synagogues and prisons, and you will be brought before kings and governors, and all on account of my name. This will result in your being witnesses to them. But make up your mind not to worry beforehand how you will defend yourselves. For I will give you words and wisdom that none of your adversaries will be able to resist or contradict.
(Luke 21:12-15)

Our satisfaction and protection are in God alone:

He who dwells in the shelter of the Most High will rest in the shadow of the Almighty. I will say of the LORD, "He is my refuge and my fortress, my God, in whom I trust." Surely he will save you from the fowler's snare and from the deadly pestilence. He will cover you with his feathers, and under his wings you will find refuge; His faithfulness will be your shield and rampart. You will not fear the terror of night, nor the arrow that flies by day, nor the pestilence that stalks in the darkness, nor the plague that destroys at midday. A thousand may fall at your side, ten thousand at your right hand, but it will not come near you. You will only observe with your eyes and see the punishment of the wicked.

If you make the Most High your dwelling— even the LORD, who is my refuge- then no harm will befall you, no disaster will come near your tent. For he will command his angels concerning you to guard you in all your ways; they will lift you up in their hands, so that you will not strike your foot against a stone. You will tread upon the lion and the cobra; you will trample the great lion and the serpent. "Because he loves me," says the LORD, "I will rescue him; I will protect him, for he acknowledges my name. He will call upon me, and I will answer him; I will be with him in trouble, I will deliver him and honor him. With long life will I satisfy him and show him my salvation. (Psalm 91)

God will deliver us from all fears:

I sought the LORD, and he answered me; He delivered me from all my fears. (Psalm 34:4)

God is our FIREWALL:

And I myself will be a wall of fire around it,' declares the LORD, 'and I will be its glory within.' (Zechariah 2:5)

We can resist being afraid because God is with us:

TheLORD is with me; I will not be afraid. What can man do to me? (Psalm 118:6)

The Holy Spirit will speak through us:

"Whatever town or village you enter, search for some worthy person there and stay at his house until you leave. As you enter the home, give it your greeting. If the home is deserving, let your peace rest on it; if it is not, let your peace return to you.

If anyone will not welcome you or listen to your words, shake the dust off your feet when you leave that home or town. I tell you the truth, it will be more bearable for Sodom and Gomorrah on the day of judgment than for that town. I am sending you out like sheep among wolves.

Therefore be as shrewd as snakes and as innocent as doves. "Be on your guard against men; they will hand you over to the local councils and flog you in their synagogues.

On my account you will be brought before governors and kings as witnesses to them and to the Gentiles. But when they arrest you, do not worry about what to say or how to say it.

At that time you will be given what to say, for it will not be you speaking, but the Spirit of your Father speaking through you. (Matthew 10:11-20)

Do not fear, God has called you and He will be with you, He will protect you:

"But you, O Israel, my servant, Jacob, whom I have chosen, you descendants of Abraham my friend, I took you from the ends of the earth, from its farthest corners I called you.
I said, 'You are my servant'; I have chosen you and have not rejected you. So do not fear, for I am with you; do not be dismayed, for I am your God. I will strengthen you and help you; I will uphold you with my righteous right hand. "All who rage against you will surely be ashamed and disgraced; those who oppose you will be as nothing and perish. Though you search for your enemies, you will not find them. Those who wage war against you will be as nothing at all. For I am the LORD, your God, who takes hold of your right hand and says to you, 'Do not fear; I will help you.'" (Isaiah 41:8-13)

Real love for sinners takes away our fear:

There is no fear in love. But perfect love drives out fear, because fear has to do with punishment. The one who fears is not made perfect in love. (1 John 4:18)

So get ready; stand up and do not be terrified:

"Get yourself ready! Stand up and say to them whatever I command you. Do not be terrified by them, or I will terrify you before them." (Jeremiah 1:17)

"Now go; I will help you speak and will teach you what to say." (Exodus 4:12)

But the LORD is with me like a mighty warrior; so my persecutors will stumble and not prevail. They will fail and be thoroughly disgraced; their dishonor will never be forgotten. (Jeremiah 20:11)

RECOGNIZE THE RESULTS OF PERSECUTION

The results of persecution go beyond the immediate physical and natural experience. Persecution advances the Kingdom of God:

Now I want you to know, brothers, that what has happened to me has really served to advance the gospel. As a result, it has become clear throughout the whole palace guard and to everyone else that I am in chains for Christ.

Because of my chains, most of the brothers in the Lord have been encouraged to speak the word of God more courageously and fearlessly.

For I know that through your prayers and the help given by the Spirit of Jesus Christ, what has happened to me will turn out for my deliverance. (Philippians 1:12-14, 19)

In Vietnam, under communism, there are no chaplains in the prisons, but through my prison time, many prisoners and guards had a chance to hear the Gospel. I led many prisoners to the Lord and started many churches in the prisons. My wife visited the families of the new Christians and led them to the Lord, as well.

This encouraged many people in the Church in Vietnam to share the Gospel fearlessly, since I did so even in prison. As a result, the Church doubled in size. This would not have happened if I had not been imprisoned for the sake of the Gospel. During my imprisonments, many Christians around the world learned about my persecution and prayed for me.

We turn mourning into dancing; *Baca* into sweet; sorrow into joy:

Blessed are those whose strength is in you, who have set their hearts on pilgrimage. As they pass through the Valley of Baca, they make it a place of springs; the autumn rains also cover it with pools. They go from strength to strength, till each appears before God in Zion. (Psalm 84:5-7)

We grow in character and joy:

James, a servant of God and of the Lord Jesus Christ, to the twelve tribes scattered among the nations: Greetings. Consider it pure joy, my brothers, whenever you face trials of many kinds, because you know that the testing of your faith develops perseverance. (James 1:1-3)

Our faith is purified and becomes more worthy than gold:

Praise be to the God and Father of our Lord Jesus Christ! In his great mercy he has given us new birth into a living hope through the resurrection of Jesus Christ from the dead, and into an inheritance that can never perish, spoil or fade—kept in heaven for you, who through faith are shielded by God's power until the coming of the salvation that is ready to be revealed in the last time.

In this you greatly rejoice, though now for a little while you may have had to suffer grief in all kinds of trials. These have come so that your faith—of greater worth than gold, which perishes even though refined by fire—may be proved genuine and may result in praise, glory and honor when Jesus Christ is revealed.Though you have not seen him, you love him; and even though you do not see him now, you believe in him and are filled with an inexpressible and glorious joy, for you are receiving the goal of your faith, the salvation of your souls. (1 Peter 1:3-9)

We confirm our testimony to the world about Who we believe in:

Grace and peace to you from God our Father and the Lord Jesus Christ. I always thank God for you because of his grace given you in Christ Jesus.

For in him you have been enriched in every way—in all your speaking and in all your knowledge— because our testimony about Christ was confirmed in you.

Therefore you do not lack any spiritual gift as you eagerly wait for our Lord Jesus Christ to be revealed. He will keep you strong to the end, so that you will be blameless on the day of our Lord Jesus Christ.

God, who has called you into fellowship with his Son Jesus Christ our Lord, is faithful. (I Corinthians 1:3-9)

We build our reward in heaven:

Blessed are you when people insult you, persecute you and falsely say all kinds of evil against you because of me. Rejoice and be glad, because great is your reward in heaven, for in the same way they persecuted the prophets who were before you. (Matthew 5:11-12)

Our life example will cause sinners to turn from sin:

Remember this: Whoever turns a sinner from the error of his way will save him from death and cover over a multitude of sins. (James 5:20)

Laying down our life causes others to know Him:

This is how we know what love is: Jesus Christ laid down his life for us. And we ought to lay down our lives for our brothers. (1 John 3:16)

STORY OF SISTER TAI

Sister Tai planted a church right after she graduated from Bible school. Within a short time of starting the church, she was arrested and put in jail. She was in jail for four months before being released because they could not find any evidence with which to charge her.

A year later, the police captain of the town in which she lived and was arrested came to look for her. He said, "I have kept my eye on you, and see that you have started a church in the village. I notice that the church is growing and that the criminal activity has decreased in our town. I want to be a part of your church."

Sister Tai replied, "You must be kidding me!" "No, I'm serious," he replied. "Well, if you're serious, then you must resign as the police captain, quit your job, come to the church, repent and accept the Lord as your Savior. Then, you must go to three months discipleship to prepare for water baptism, and then you can join the church."

"Wow, that is so difficult," he said. "Well, no, actually the most difficult decision has already been done for you," she said, referring to the fact that Jesus died for him. "Give me a couple weeks to think about that," he said.

After two weeks, he came back, "Well, I have thought carefully about this. Not only am I going to resign from my position and quit my job as the police captain and do what you said to become a member of the church, I also want to…"

A little surprised that he had made the decision to give up his position and to follow Jesus, Sister Tai interrupted him, "What else do you want to do?"

"I want to marry you!" he said. She could not believe what she was hearing and told him, "You have got to be kidding me, now!"

"No, I'm serious," he said. She replied, "Well, that's not going to be easy, either. I am not going to give myself to anyone who is not a disciple of Jesus." "I am going to follow Jesus," the police captain reassured her.

Sister Tai went on to explain, "In addition to resigning from your job, repenting and accepting Jesus as Lord and Savior, attending three months of discipleship, and being baptized, you need to go to my church for two years, and pay your tithes and offerings before we will talk about the next step."

So, the former police captain did all that Sister Tai said, and two years later they called me and asked me to marry them. I said, "Yes, but you need to go through my counseling first, and I make it really tough." They agreed, and so we started the pre-marital counseling sessions.

During our meetings, I asked many difficult questions and instructed them on the meaning and commitment of marriage.During one session I asked the former police chief, "Why did you quit your job and your career and want to marry this crazy lady?"

He told me, "Well pastor, you may not know this, but as the police captain I watched her when she was in prison, and there was no one else like her. Even in prison, all religious leaders eventually turn into human beings after one month. But this lady is different.

She walks the way she talks. She loves, she cares, and she shares with people, even under the harsh conditions of prison. So, I knew she was the best wife I could find."

After they got married, they started planting churches together. While his wife preaches, he stands guard. During one of the services, the police came to arrest his wife. They were surprised to see their former chief. "What are you doing here, chief?" they asked. "I'm on duty," he told them. "What's your duty?" "I am taking care of my wife," he replied. "Oh, we came to arrest her." "You're crazy. Get out of here! I'm her bodyguard now," he told them.

Sister Taiis a powerful example of how persecution is used as a witness to unbelievers.

STORY OF BROTHER SEVEN

Brother Seven was the chief of security in a village in central VN. He arrested and persecuted many Christians in his village. He would have each person interrogated and then a report written on each one. Since he was the chief security officer, he read all the reports. As he read the reports, he began to see the courage and conviction of the Christians. They were strong and would do anything for their God.

Less than a year later, he called all the village citizens together. He instructed all the Christians to sit on the right side, and all the people that were not believers to sit on the left side. The Christians were really wondering what he was planning. They waited nervously to learn what would happen next. Surely, he is going to persecute them, they thought. "Tonight is my last night as a chief security officer of this village," he announced. To everyone's amazement, he also announced, "I am going to join the Christian group."

As a result of reading the reports and watching the Christians he persecuted, he was drawn to Christ. He accepted Jesus as his Lord and Savior. Shortly afterward, he interviewed with me to attend our Bible school. After his Bible school training, he went back to his village to win souls.

Because of his bold testimony and evangelizing, he was arrested and tortured by the very officers that had worked under him before. He told them, "Friends, I am not angry with you. I am reaping what I sowed for many years when I persecuted the Christians. Today, I want you all to receive Jesus Christ as your Lord and Savior, so that you will not reap what is happening to me today." They continued to beat him and torture him so severely that he had to be put in the hospital for about a month. After that, he became so on fire for the Lord and went on to plant many churches in central highlands of Vietnam.

FOLLOW THE EXAMPLES OF PEOPLE
IN THE BIBLE

We can learn how to face persecution from examples in the Bible.Jesus experienced extreme mental, physical, emotional, and spiritual persecution as He suffered and died for us:

One of the criminals who hung there hurled insults at him: "Aren't you the Christ? Save yourself and us!" But the other criminal rebuked him. "Don't you fear God," he said, "since you are under the same sentence? We are punished justly, for we are getting what our deeds deserve. But this man has done nothing wrong."

Then he said, "Jesus, remember me when you come into your kingdom." Jesus answered him, "I tell you the truth, today you will be with me in paradise." (Luke 23:39-43)

Just as Jesus did, Stephen was able to forgive his persecutors as they stoned him to death:

Then he fell on his knees and cried out, "Lord, do not hold this sin against them." When he had said this, he fell asleep. (Acts 7:60)

Paul experienced desertion from his friends, yet he was able to forgive them:

At my first defense, no one came to my support, but everyone deserted me. May it not be held against them. (II Timothy 4:16)

OTHER THINGS WE ARE TO DO

The Bible gives us specific commands when we face persecution. Our job is to pray for and actively love our enemies and people who persecute us. Revenge for ill-treatment should be left up to God:

But I tell you: Love your enemies and pray for those who persecute you, that you may be sons of your Father in heaven. He causes his sun to rise on the evil and the good, and sends rain on the righteous and the unrighteous. (Matthew 5:44-45)

Bless those who persecute you; bless and do not curse. Rejoice with those who rejoice; mourn with those who mourn. Live in harmony with one another. Do not be proud, but be willing to associate with people of low position. Do not be conceited. Do not repay anyone evil for evil. Be careful to do what is right in the eyes of everybody. If it is possible, as far as it depends on you, live at peace with everyone.

Do not take revenge, my friends, but leave room for God's wrath, for it is written: "It is mine to avenge; I will repay," says the Lord.

On the contrary: "If your enemy is hungry, feed him; if he is thirsty, give him something to drink. In doing this, you will heap burning coals on his head." Do not be overcome by evil, but overcome evil with good. (Romans 12:14-19)

Persecution is difficult to endure, but when we recognize that through our persecution Christ is glorified, we are purified, and sinners are saved, then we can be encouraged that our persecution will not be in vain. We are not alone in the persecution.

Many people have endured and overcome persecution in the past; many are currently enduring and overcoming; and many will endure and overcome in the future. Jesus is with us and will strengthen us if we stand fast, obey, and encourage ourselves in His Word.

POWER OF
PRAYER & FASTING | 19

Fasting and prayer have a powerful effect in the spiritual realm that most Christians do not realize. These disciplines are even exercised in the kingdom of darkness as tools to empower demonic forces. If Christians realized what happens in the spiritual realm when they fast and pray with the authority of the Kingdom of God, then they would not be inclined to treat them so lightly.

When Jesus sent his disciples, he said that he was sending them as sheep going among wolves – *Matthew 10:16* and *Luke 10:3*. This means we are sent into an evil world, but we are to remain righteous. He wants to send us into the world to bring people out of darkness into light, from Satan unto God. In *Acts 26:16-18*, God told Saul (later named Paul) that He was sending him *"to open their eyes and turn them from darkness to light, and from the power of Satan to God...."*

We know that God sends us into the dark places, the places controlled by various devils. In *Matthew 12:29*, Jesus said that before we can go into a house, we must first bind the strongman. The devil is the strongman that controls this world. As God's disciples, we are sent into the world to take back what the devil has taken.

Our ministry is to take people from the kingdom of darkness into the kingdom of God. This is not an easy thing to do, but fasting and praying gives us power.During the time of Jesus, John the Baptist's disciples fasted all the time; however, they did not have faith during the time of their fasting. Fasting must go together with faith.

In *Matthew 17:21*, Jesus instructed His disciples that unless they fasted and prayed they could not drive out that demon.So, fasting and praying is vital to being able to deal with evil spirits. We are called to deal with the power of Satan, and we cannot do it with our own strength, knowledge, and experience – we need to depend on God! This is the reason why the Church needs to not only pray, but to also fast.

In *Mark 2:20*, Jesus said that when the bridegroom is with you, you do not need to fast; but when the bridegroom is not with you, you need to fast and pray. This is why we need to fast and pray, now, since Jesus is not with us. I believe this is what the disciples were doing when they were in the Upper Room in *Acts 1*. They were praying and fasting, since Jesus (the Bridegroom) was no longer with them.

Today, we need to be filled with the Holy Spirit so that we can deal with evil spirits. In *Mark 16:17*, Jesus said that we would drive out demons in His name.

In many cases, fasting and praying enables us to walk in and exercise the authority and power to drive out demons, to bind the strongman and take back what has been stolen from the Kingdom of God. Unless you fast, you cannot deal with the demons.

In Vietnam, I required all the pastors under me to meet together with at least six other pastors in their district every Friday to fast and pray for the ministry in their district. On Saturday, they were required to meet with their church members to fast and pray for their church.

On July 7, 1988, we experienced a strong move of the Holy Spirit. It was during a time of prayer and fasting. The Holy Spirit was so strong that as soon as anyone – Pentecostal, anti-Pentecostal, etc. – walked into the room, they were touched by the power of the Holy Spirit, filled with the Holy Spirit and would begin to speak in tongues; and signs, wonders and miracles began to happen. This move of the Holy Spirit began to knock down the walls of tradition and denominations in Vietnam.

As a witchdoctor I fasted and prayed against many of the missionaries that came to our area, and was very successful in stopping their work. When I tried this with the group of missionaries that came to my town in 1970, it failed. I found out later that they were fasting and praying missionaries.

None of my gods could stand against the power of the Holy Spirit when these missionaries fasted and prayed. I soon discovered that the power of the Holy Spirit was greater than the power of my demonic gods. It is vital as Christians to fast and pray in order to be successful in spiritual warfare, there is no way that you can use your own knowledge, your own experience to fight against the powers of darkness.

As a result of the Christians fasting and praying in Vietnam, the underground Church has really grown and has a strong foundation for fasting and prayer. They continue to operate in signs, wonders, and miracles.

If you want to win the battle, you must learn to fast and pray. If you want to drive out demons and gain ground for the Kingdom of God, you must fast and pray.

I was born into a very wealthy family, but they sent me to be trained as a Buddhist monk so that I could learn how to live a simple, sacrificial life. When I left Buddhism at age fifteen, I became a witchdoctor. As a witchdoctor, I became very wealthy, even more so than my family. I was one of the highest witchdoctors of my town and became very popular for being able to bless and curse what people wanted.

In the evil spirit world, your faith depends on your heart, and your heart depends on your wallet. As a witchdoctor, people would ask me to perform miracles for them, but I would never tell them a price. InsteadI would say, "Your heart will define how big your miracle will be. If you want a big miracle, then the bigger the offering you should invest (sow)."

So, when people came to me, they would give a lot because they expected a big miracle. As a result, I became very wealthy. I had more money than my grandfather who was a medical doctor, and more money than my dad who was chief (mayor) of the town. An example of this practise is given in the Bible in *Acts 8:18-19*when Simon the sorcerer tried to buy the power of the Holy Spirit.

When I became a Christian, I was disowned by my family and community, so of course, I no longer had people giving me offerings for miracles, and I became very poor.

When I went to Bible school, I had to work very hard to pay for housing, food and tuition. I washed cars, cleaned the bathrooms, and was a guard in the evenings. After Bible school, I became a pastor and was still very poor. My friends were shocked, "How can this guy who was a witchdoctor become this poor?"

I was happy though, because the doctrine being taught at that time was that the more you are poor and the more you suffer, the more holy you are. So for fifteen years, I lived in poverty.When my ministry got bigger, many people in business and high position who were wealthy came to me for help. They saw the poverty in which I lived and could not understand.

This caused me to ask God, "Why? I am an ambassador and prince of the heavenly kingdom doing Your work to present Your kingdom to this world. How can I be this poor?" The Holy Spirit answered me, "You have not because you ask not." I said, "No, I do ask."

He told me, "You ask but you do not believe. You believe in a life of poverty. You do not believe in a life of prosperity." I was shocked. The Holy Spirit told me, "Okay, turn in your Bible to Mark chapter 10, start from verses 28 and go to verse 30. Peter asked the same question."

So I began to read, *"'I tell you the truth,' Jesus replied, 'no one who has left home or brothers or sisters or mother or father or children or fields for me and the gospel will fail to receive a hundredfold as much in this present age (homes, brothers, sisters, mothers, children and fields – and with them persecutions) and in the age to come, eternal life.'"* I was really shocked.

I read it over and over again. "What does it mean, *hundredfold*? What does it mean, *with persecution*? Who would persecute me if I am rich?" *Eternity* was easy to believe, because every religion has promises about eternity. "But what does it mean *hundredfold in this world*?" This really shocked me. I read it over and over because I did not understand.

"Can God really give me hundredfold in this world?" I was trained that you have to be poor to be holy, now I read that God can give me hundredfold in this world, and persecution.

I decided to take three months to study what the Bible has to say about prosperity. I wanted to know two things: 1) Can I really be prosperous in this world, receiving hundredfold before I get to heaven? I thought hundredfold was for when I get to heaven. 2) If I am prosperous, who is going to persecute me?

For three months, I read the Bible three times to find out if these promises were Biblical. When I got started I suddenly remembered one of the verses I always preached to people, Jeremiah 29:11, *"'For I know the plans I have for you,' declares the Lord, 'plans to prosper you and not to harm you, plans to give you hope and a future.'"*

God also told Abram in Genesis 12:2, *"I will make you into a great nation and I will bless you; I will make your name great, and you will be a blessing.'"*

While I was wondering whether this was still God's plan for His children, I was reminded of Joshua 1:8, *"'Do not let this Book of the law depart from your mouth; meditate on it day and night, so that you may be careful to do everything written in it. Then you will be prosperous and successful.'"*

Then I read verse seven, where God says, *"Be strong and very courageous. Be careful to obey all the law my servant Moses gave you; do not turn from it to the right or to the left, that you may be successful wherever you go."*

I continued to search for the truth of being prosperous. I learned in *Genesis 24 and 26* that God blessed Isaac, even though the people around him did not have anything. God gave Isaac more than a hundredfold. He became very prosperous and successful, even in the time of famine.

In *Genesis 39*, we read about Joseph. Even though he was in prison, God blessed him and prospered him in everything he did. It is biblical that we will be blessed, successful and prosperous wherever we are, even in prison. God will bless and prosper us in everything that we do.

In *Exodus 1*, the Israelite midwives refused to kill the male babies as they had been instructed by the Pharaoh.

They respected God and believed in His word more than the word of the Pharaoh. Because of that, God prospered them in everything.

In *Second Samuel 5:12*, David acknowledged that God had raised him up as king over Israel. God blessed him in everything. He was prosperous in everything. In Second Chronicles 1:1, the Bible also says that God made Solomon successful, that the Lord was with him.

In the New Testament, in *Acts 13:17*, it says that God blessed Israel even while they were in Egypt. God's plan is to bless and prosper His children.

Each year on the first day of the Vietnamese New Year, the Church in Vietnam always comes together and everyone reads or recites *Psalm 1*. In verse three, the promise is that God will prosper you in everything, *"He is like a tree planted by streams of water, which yields its fruit in season and whose leaf does not wither. Whatever he does prospers."*

*Isaiah 53,*describes that as a result of His death for us, Jesus would see His successors be prosperous in everything through Him. In this chapter, we see that God gave us the full Gospel through Jesus Christ: our minds can have peace; our bodies can be healed and healthy; our spirit can be forgiven, cleansed, and ready for heaven; and our lives can be prosperous. The death and resurrection of Jesus was for our entire being – our mind, soul, spirit, body, and life.

In *Third John 2*, we see a prayer that we will prosper in everything – in our body in the same way that we prosper in our soul. In Dr. Yonggi Cho's church, Yoido Full Gospel, this verse is prominently displayed in very large letters on the wall in the church foyer as a reminder that God will prosper you in everything.

In *Deuteronomy 28*, we read in verse 12, God promises to bless everything that our hand touches, not just be blessed in our spirit. In reading this chapter, we see that God promises to make us the head and not the tail, that we will not have to borrow anything, that we will be able to loan to people, be able to bless people. This is what God intends for His children.

Since God intends for His children to be blessed, why is it that so many of them are not blessed? I continued to search the Bible. In *Joshua 1*, God said that you have to have courage to believe in God's Word. The problem of many Christians today is that they do not really believe God's Word. When we read through the Bible, we will see that God intends to bless His children. In *Genesis 1*, when God created the world, it shows that He prepared everything <u>before</u> He created man and woman.

He then created man and woman, and in verses 28-31, He instructed Adam and Eve to manage His creation. One of God's purposes for mankind is to manage what He has given us. He gave us the authority and instruction to manage the things that He created.

In *Psalm 112:1-3*, God said that all the riches that He has created will be in the house of the righteous, and in the house of their children. He will prosper those who delight in His commands: *"Praise the Lord. Blessed is the man who fears the Lord, who finds great delight in his commands. His children will be mighty in the land; the generation of the upright will be blessed. Wealth and riches are in his house, and his righteousness endures forever."*

Proverbs 8:17-21, *"I love those who love me, and those who seek me find me. With me are riches and honor, enduring wealth and prosperity. My fruit is better than fine gold; what I yield surpasses choice silver. I walk in the way of righteousness, along the paths of justice, bestowing wealth on those who love me and making their treasuries full."*

Malachi 3:10, *"'Bring the whole tithe into the storehouse, that there may be food in my house. Test me in this,' says the Lord Almighty, 'and see if I will not throw open the floodgates of heaven and pour out so much blessing that you will not have room enough for it.'"* When a floodgate is opened, it allows more water to flow into the area. When God opens the floodgates of heaven to bless us, He says that we have no room to store it. If we do not have room to store it, what can we do but to give it away? Many Christians today do not give away because they do not have, which is a problem.

In *John 10:10*, Jesus said, *"The thief comes only to steal and kill and destroy; I have come that they may have life, and have it to the full."* The thief in this verse is not the devil. If you read carefully in John 9, you will realize that the thief is really the Pharisees, the religious leaders.

Through their rules, regulations, and traditions they had stolen the best that God prepared for His children. Today, it is much the same way in that the traditions, constitutions, by-laws, theology, and doctrine of many churches and denominations keep God's children from receiving all of His blessings.

We need to remember that we serve a God that performs miracles for His children. In *John 2*, Jesus performed the miracle of turning water into wine. He turned the water into the best wine. Normally, the best wine is brought out at the beginning of the celebration. Then, when people are drunk, the lower quality wine is brought out because people will not recognize that the wine is not as good. Jesus, however, only gave the best. When Jesus performs a miracle, He will give you the best miracle.

In *Matthew 14, Mark 6, Luke 9, John 6*, Jesus fed at least five thousand men and thousands more women and children with only five loaves of bread and two fish. After everyone ate until they were satisfied, there were twelve baskets of food left over.

This shows that when Jesus performs a miracle, it is more than enough, it is overflowing. This is an example of how he gives in abundance.

In Matthew 7:9-11, Jesus says, *"'Which of you, if his son asks for bread, will give him a stone? Or if he asks for a fish, will give him a snake? If you, then, though you are evil, know how to give good gifts to your children, how much more will your Father in heaven give good gifts to those who ask him!'"*

Even the wicked know how to give good gifts to their children, so how much more will a loving heavenly Father give the best to those who ask Him? God our heavenly Father will always give us good gifts, even better than what we are expecting. He will always give His children what is best for them. Many Christians are stingy so they think God is stingy, so they really do not want to give.

In *Matthew 6:2, 5 and 16*, Jesus talks about giving, praying and fasting. He begins each teaching with the phrase, "'When you give...,' 'When you pray...,' 'When you fast....'" He says "when," not "if." This shows that giving is a part of the ordinary, normal, regular life of a disciple of Jesus. The keys of the kingdom are giving, praying and fasting.

Unfortunately, many churches today focus a lot on prayer, but they forget the first thing that Jesus mentioned was giving. They put prayer and fasting as first and second, and giving as third. Yet Jesus mentioned giving as coming before prayer and fasting.

To God, giving is important. He demonstrates this in *John 3:16* by giving His very best, *"For God so loved the world that he gave his one and only Son, that whoever believes in him shall not perish but have eternal life."*

According to giving, God promised that He will give us better than what we see in this world. Look at verses 26, and 28-30 in *Matthew 6*:

"Look at the birds of the air; they do not sow or reap or store away in barns and yet your heavenly Father feeds them. Are you not much more valuable than they? ...And why do you worry about clothes? See how the lilies of the field grow. They do not labor or spin. Yet I tell you that not even Solomon in all his splendor was dressed like one of these. If that is how God clothes the grass of the field, which is here today and tomorrow is thrown into the fire, will he not much more clothe you, O you of little faith?'"

Jesus said that the flowers of the field were dressed even better than Solomon who was the richest person in the world at the time. Are we not better than flowers and the birds? God will provide all of our needs according to His riches, not according to our poverty.

His plans for us are according to Jeremiah 29:11, *"'For I know the plans that I have for you,' declares the Lord, 'plans to prosper you and not to harm you, plans to give you hope and a future.'"*

People say that Jesus was poor, so we must be poor, but that is not true. Jesus became poor so that we could be rich. Look at Second Corinthians 8:9, *"For you know the grace of our Lord Jesus Christ, that though he was rich, yet for your sakes he became poor, so that you through his poverty might become rich."*

God intends to bless us so that we can be a blessing to others, including our families. It is a poor testimony if we do not take care of our family. In First Timothy 5:8, Paul wrote, *"If anyone does not provide for his relatives, and especially for his immediate family, he has denied the faith and is worse than an unbeliever."* I have seen many people in Vietnam and other parts of the world who lack God's truth and do not provide for their families.

In Cambodia, I spoke with a pastor's son who said he never wanted to be a pastor because he did not want to be poor. He went on to explain that he asked his father for a CD player, since all his friends in class had MP3 players.

When he asked his father, he replied, "Son, you know I am a pastor. How can I have money to buy you a CD player?" His son said, "Dad, you are an ambassador of the heavenly kingdom, and the dads of the kids in my class are only businessmen.

They have already bought them MP3 and MP4 players, and have gotten rid of their CD players. Dad, you are an ambassador of God, and you tell me you do not have money to buy me even a CD player. So, why don't you quit serving God's kingdom and become a business man so that you can provide for your children?" I have heard similar stories all over the world. We have not grasped the truth and principles of God's Word, and the result is that we do not live as prosperous children of God.

In Matthew 7:7-8, Jesus said, *"'Ask and it will be given to you; seek, and you will find; knock and the door will be opened to you. For everyone who asks receives; he who seeks finds; and to him who knocks, the door will be opened.'"* He continues on in verses 9-12 to describe that even wicked fathers can give good gifts to their children, so, how much more will God give good gifts to His children?

Many people think that the Church is supposed to be poor. This is not true. We are instructed in Malachi 3:10 to bring the entire tithe into the storehouse sothat there will be lack of nothing, so that there will be plenty. Many churches today have financial difficulty because people do not obey the Bible by bringing their tithes into the storehouse.

We are also instructed in *Galatians 6:6* to bring the best to the people who teach us. Paul goes on in verse seven to explain that we will reap whatever we sow.

I have seen, however, in many churches that when people bring furniture, clothing, and other things to the church for the church to give away, the pastor's spouse and children are the first ones to go through it because they are too poor to be able to buy things for themselves.

This is contrary to what we are admonished to do. In First Timothy 5:17-18, Paul says, *"The elders who direct the affairs of the church well are worthy of double honor, especially those whose work is preaching and teaching. For the Scripture says, 'Do not muzzle the ox while it is treading out the grain,' and 'The worker deserves his wages.'"*

Paul tells us to treat our leaders with double honor, yet in the Church today we do not treat our leaders as such. For example, a person who has a doctorate degree can work for the world and make $150,000 each year. This same person working as the president of a Bible college would only be able to make half of this amount.

Yet, Paul tells us that they are worth double what the world's standards are. This means that the Church gives its leaders only 25% of what Paul says they should receive, since Paul's standards are double of what the world's standards are.

If we cannot love and care for those who are taking care of us, who teach us, pray for us, stand beside us, then how can we love the sinner who cares nothing for us?

It is hypocritical to say that we love unbelievers when we do not love and honor those who are our pastors and leaders. So, we must provide first for our families, secondly for our pastors and leaders, and then for the church.

Romans 10:14-15 is familiar to many people, *"How, then, can they call on the one they have not believed in? And how can they believe in the one of whom they have not heard? And how can they hear without someone preaching to them? And how can they preach unless they are sent? As it is written, 'How beautiful are the feet of those who bring good news!'"*

We like to talk about, "How beautiful are the feet of those who bring good news!" What we forget is that those who bring the good news must be sent in order for people to hear the gospel. If we do not go, and we do not send, we are not being obedient.

Over the years, the Church is sending less and less because Christians are lacking money to provide for their families, for their leaders, and in their churches for evangelism.In *Haggai 1:5-11*, we see that we can prevent the blessing of God in our lives when the house of God is neglected. In Vietnam, and in some other places, people are more focused on the size of their house than the size of the church building. This is representative of people's hearts being more interested in providing the best for themselves while neglecting the house of God.

BREAKING THE CURSE OF POVERTY

We can break the curse of poverty by following the principles of giving. Jesus taught us that when we give, it will be given back again to us,

"Give, and it will be given to you. A good measure, pressed down, shaken together and running over, will be poured into your lap. For with the measure you use, it will be measured to you." (Luke 6:38)

In *II Corinthians 9:6-13,* Paul writes to the Corinthian church about sowing and reaping. Today, many people interpret this to mean sowing the Gospel, but when you read this chapter carefully you can see that Paul is not referring to sowing the Gospel. He is writing about the matter of sowing finances in these verses.

Remember this: Whoever shows sparingly will also reap sparingly, and whoever sows generously will also reap generously. Each man should give what he has decided in his heart to give, not reluctantly or under compulsion, for God loves a cheerful giver. And God is able to make all grace abound to you, so that in all things at all times, having all that you need, you will abound in every good work.

As it is written: "He has scattered abroad his gifts to the poor; his righteousness endures forever."

Now he who supplies seed to the sower and bread for food will also supply and increase your store of seed and will enlarge the harvest of your righteousness. You will be made rich in every way so that you can be generous on every occasion, and through us your generosity will result in thanksgiving to God.

KNOWING WHERE TO SOW YOUR SEED

To "sow" is to plant seed into the ground in order to reap, or get back, a harvest. When seed is sown, it goes into the soil. If the soil is good, then the seed will grow and will yield a harvest that is greater than the seed that was planted. Mark chapter four has Jesus' Parable of the Sower, which describes the value of sowing into good soil. Of course there are many opportunities to give within the Church, so we need to understand what the Bible considers "good soil."

First, we must understand that an offering is considered to be separate from our tithe. The first thing that we are supposed to give is our tithe. The tithe is required to go to the local church where we attend, as described in Malachi:

Bring the whole tithe into the storehouse, that there may be food in my house. Test me in this,' says the Lord Almighty, 'and see if I will not throw open the floodgates of heaven and pour out so much blessing that you will not have room enough for it. (Malachi 3:10)

Anything above our tithe is considered an offering, and there are many different kinds of offerings described in the Bible. When giving our offering, we need to consider the "soil" into which it is being sown. It is the same concept of investing our finances into companies and savings that give a good return on our investments.

Just as it is not wise use of our money to invest into a bankrupt company or into a savings plan is likely to fail, sowing our finances into the kingdom of God follows the same principles.

The first thing to remember is that God makes provision for an offering. In Genesis 22:6-18, Abraham was willing to offer his son Isaac as an offering to God. He knew that God would provide, even if it seemed that his obedience to God meant the end of what God had promised through Isaac.

Just as Abraham was going to kill his son, God provided a ram for the offering. Abraham had proven himself willing to give up what was most precious to him in obedience to God. It was never God's intention for Abraham to slay his son as the offering. At that moment God gave provision for the offering to be made. So, this shows us that God even provides the means for us to make an offering to Him.

Many Christians have memorized Philippians 4:19, *"And my God will meet all your needs according to his glorious riches in Christ Jesus."* It is a great verse of promise; however, they forget to look at the verses before it to understand why Paul was writing to the Philippian Christians.

Moreover, as you Philippians know, in the early days of your acquaintance with the gospel, when I set out from Macedonia, not one church shared with me in the matter of giving and receiving, except you only; for even when I was in Thessalonica, you sent me aid again and again when I was in need. Not that I am looking for a gift, but I am looking for what may be credited to your account. I have received full payment and even more; I am amply supplied, now that I have received from Epaphroditus the gifts you sent. They are a fragrant offering, an acceptable sacrifice, pleasing to God. And my God will meet all your need according to his glorious riches in Christ Jesus. (Philippians 4:15-19)

When Paul went to the new mission field to win souls and start churches, the Philippian church was the only church that sowed finances to help with these efforts. They sowed into the mission work that Paul was doing. Paul was not asking for finances. He had already learned that God would provide for his needs, and he had learned to be content in all circumstances. (See *Phil. 4:11*) He was commending the Philippians on their giving to missions because their giving was actually a benefit to them.

Paul went on to explain that God would provide all their needs out of His riches. The needs of people are different, and God is not poor. He is able to treat you as a prince or princess, as an ambassador of His heavenly kingdom. He is able to give you a harvest according to the seed that you sow.

This is why I am not stingy to sow the seed. I want to have a better harvest, to be treated as a wealthy child of the King, an ambassador of the heavenly kingdom. If I am stingy, I am not allowing God's abundance to operate in my life. In Paul's description of the benefits of sowing into missions, we can see that missions is a very sound investment of the financial seed that we sow into God's kingdom. We will reap God's blessing in this life, and will be investing into the eternal Kingdom of God.

I like what Dr. Yonggi Cho teaches the people in his church in Korea. He tells them, "The day you became a Christian was the last day that you had to live in poverty. From that point forward, you are a child of God, and God wants to treat you as a prince or a princess. So, prepare yourself and behave and act like you are a prince or princess of the heavenly kingdom."

I shared this with people that were saved in our churches in Vietnam. Many of them were living in the street when they came to the Lord, and now they live in three-story houses. It all comes from God because they know how to sow the seed.

They began to behave like children of the King, and so they were able to receive the blessings of being a child of the King.

Some people ask me whether they can use God's money to support other ministries such as giving to television ministries. I tell them, "Yes, of course, after you pay your tithe and invest in missions. You know, when you are in the hospital, the television cannot visit you. When you are facing a divorce, the television cannot counsel you and restore your marriage. When you die, the television cannot come to perform your funeral. So, you really need to find out which ministry is a benefit to your life and your walk with God the most and give to that."

People ask me whether they can give to the poor. I agree that we need to give to the poor, as well as help provide a way for them to get out of their poverty. God even tells us to give to the poor.

He who has pity on the poor lends to the Lord, and that which he has given He will repay to him.
(Proverbs 19:17, Amplified)

He who gives to the poor will not want, but he who hides his eyes [from their want] will have many a curse.
(Proverbs 28:27, Amplified)

Notice that the money that we give to the poor is a loan to God rather than an investment. When you loan money, you receive that same amount back.

If you give $100, then you will get back $100. So, giving to the poor does not necessarily give you an increase in your finances.Our priorities in giving should be to tithe first, and then give to missions.

HOW MUCH SHOULD I GIVE?

And now, brothers, we want you to know about the grace that God has given the Macedonian churches. Out of the most severe trial, their overflowing joy and their extreme poverty welled up in rich generosity. For I testify that they gave as much as they were able, and even beyond their ability. Entirely on their own, they urgently pleaded with us for the privilege of sharing in this service to the saints.

Any they did not do as we expected, but they gave themselves first to the Lord and then to us in keeping with God's will. So we urged Titus, since he had earlier made a beginning, to bring also to completion this act of grace on your part. But just as you excel in everything – in faith, in speech, in knowledge, in complete earnestness and in your love for us – see that you also excel in this grace of giving. I am not commanding you, but I want to test the sincerity of your love by comparing it with the earnestness of others.

For you know the grace of our Lord Jesus Christ, that though he was rich, yet for your sakes he became poor, so that you through his poverty might become rich.

(II Corinthians 8:1-9)

In the first verse, we see that the people gave out of their joyful heart, beyond their ability. Only you and God know what is "beyond your ability." In the midst of the problems and the hardships of the Corinthian church, they still gave above their situation.

Many times, we only give according to our situation, such as the amount of money that we have left over after we take care of the other things that we need or want. Paul is describing here that the Christians gave according to the joy that was in their hearts. They gave abundantly, even beyond what their situation allowed at the time.

One of my pastors in Vietnam gave a demonstration about giving after a lady in his church told him, "Pastor, I give and give and give, just like you teach us, but why don't I receive anything back?" The next Sunday the pastor brought two bottles of sugar and two bowls. He picked one man in the church to come forward and instructed him, "Open the top of this bottle and pour the sugar into this bowl." He then told the woman who asked him the question about giving and receiving, "Poke a hole in the top of this bottle and pour the sugar into this bowl."

It took the man only five seconds to pour all the sugar out of his bottle into the bowl, yet even after twenty-five minutes the woman had not finished squeezing all the sugar out of her bottle into the bowl.

The pastor had finished his message, so he told her that she could finish pouring the sugar out of the bottle the next week.

The following Sunday, while he was preaching, the pastor had the lady continue emptying the sugar out of the bottle through the hole in the top. By the time he finished his message, she was finished emptying the bottle. The pastor said, "Both of you have finished emptying the sugar out of the bottles. This is a symbol of how you pour money out of your wallet into an offering for God. Now it is time for God to return back to you. Put all the sugar from the bowl back into the bottle."

The man that had taken only five seconds to pour the sugar out of his bottle now took close to thirty minutes to get it back in to the bottle. It took the lady three days to get the sugar back into her bottle the same way that she poured it out through the pinhole in the top.

The pastor explained, "The same way that you open your wallet to give to the Lord is the same way that you will receive back from Him. If you open it widely to give out, then it will come back very quickly.

If you only punch a hole and try to squeeze very hard to give money out, then it will be the same way coming back to you. So, it depends the way that you give: if you give generously and easily, then it will come back to you quickly; if you give stingily and slowly, then it will come back to you the same way."

Each September in Vietnam, churches begin their Christmas fundraising campaign. People make their faith promises in September and then they begin giving in October. The amount of money that they have raised by the beginning of December determines how much they can spend on decorations and gifts for the outreach.

At the beginning of the Christmas fundraising campaign at one of the churches, an old man in the church was first to raise his hand to commit to give $50. Everyone was shocked because this man was poor and depended a lot on benevolence from the church. The next person to commit to give money in the campaign did not want to be out-given by this very poor man, so he committed to give $75. The next person gave $100, the next person $150, the next, $200, and each person wanted to out-give the person before them. As a result, they raised around $2,000 for the Christmas outreach.

By December, they noticed that the man had not given anything, even though he had made a pledge of $50. So, the Board and financial director went to visit the man at his house. The man made a big deal out of it. He said, "Oh, all you big men came to see me at my poor house. You never came to do this before. Why are you visiting me?""We have come to visit with you, pray with you, and to collect the money," they told him. "What money?" he asked, a little surprised that they would think of asking him for money. "The money that you pledged back in September for the Christmas outreach," they replied.

"Oh! How do you think I have money to give, seeing that I live on welfare and on the benevolence of the church?" They said, "Sir, you were the first one to raise your hand and promised to give $50. And because you raised your hand to give, it made other people really generous, as well."

He said, "You don't really understand, do you?" "No, we don't understand. What do you mean?" they asked. The old man told them, "My pledge was the bait. Without my $50, do you think people would have given that much money?!"

Often, people give because there is bait that was thrown out. They do not want someone to give more than them, so they give out of pride rather than love.

Going back to *II Corinthians 8*, we see that they begged Paul to allow them to have a part in giving. They gave out of a joyful heart, even beyond what was seemed naturally possible for them to do. To them, giving was an honor, a privilege, an opportunity. We need to begin to see giving the same way – as an opportunity to exercise our faith, a privilege and honor to partner with God and sow into His work.

WHAT GIVING IS NOT

Giving to God is not a means to provide for the needs of the poor. It is not social work, nor a benevolent system. Yes, we should care for the poor, but God expects us to manage our finances well or what we have will be taken away from us. *"Whoever has will be given more; whoever does not have, even what he has will be taken from him"* (Mark 4:25).

When someone is poor, it is often because he/she does not manage the amount that God has already provided for them, so what little they have is taken away.I do not give to people or ministries which are not good stewards of what they are given, who do not manage their finances well.

Oftentimes, I have pastors ask me for money because they are very poor. I tell them, "If you are poor because you do not manage your finances well, why do I want to give to you? It is like giving to a bankrupt company. I want to put my money into what is blessed and where my seed will be multiplied, so that more people can get saved and the church can grow. I will help you learn how to manage your finances according the principles in God's Word. I will not give you a fish, but I will give you what you need to fish for yourself."

I go on to explain, "I would rather give my money to a rich church rather than to a poor church." This is shocking to them so I explain, "A rich church knows how to manage God's money. That is how God can trust them and can give them more money. They are faithful with what God gives them, so they are able to be blessed with more. If you cannot be faithful with little, then how can you be faithful with more? I want to plant my money into good soil, into what will produce a good harvest."

Other churches say that they are so poor that they cannot afford to give. I tell them, "Your church is so poor that it cannot afford to give, but it can afford to rob its people. You are not only robbing God, but you are robbing the people." "What? What do you mean?" they ask. "Well, the more your church is poor, the more you need to teach people about giving and provide them opportunities to give."

In I Kings, chapter 17, in the story of the poor widow of Zarephath (*I Kings 17:7-16*) and the prophet Elijah, we see an example of the provision of God released when the widow gave even her last meal to feed Elijah. She was very poor, yet she gave to the Lord. As a result, the Lord blessed her and provided for all of her needs the rest of her life.

I continue to tell the pastors when they say that their church is too poor to give, "The poorer your people are, the more we need to train them how to give. If they give, God will give it back. And if they give their last one, God will give them what will last forever."

The Bible says that the more we give into God's kingdom, the more benefit it is to our own account. So the more we lack money, the more we need to give; because the only way to have a harvest is to sow a seed.

In Vietnam, I saw many people that live in the mountains never have a harvest because when people give them seed to sow, they eat the seed and do not have anything to plant for a harvest. As a result, they stay poor all their lives. It is the same with giving into the kingdom of God. If you never sow the seed, how can you reap a harvest? If you never give to God, He does not have anything that He can bless to return to you.

PROSPERITY IN MY OWN LIFE

After I studied about giving and prosperity, I began to teach people about it. I began to live it. My wife and I had lived in poverty for fifteen years, and one day I said to her, "We are called by God. Let's serve God. Let's be faithful to do our job, and God's faithfulness will provide for our needs. If He guides us, He will provide for us. We are His ambassadors, and if we do what He tells us, then He will take care of us."

As a result, I became very prosperous. God blessed me with a lot because He could trust me with a lot. I was a good steward of what He provided, and I was generous with what He gave me. Instead of eating the seed or keeping it for myself, I sowed the seed. The result was a harvest of blessing that I could continue to give away.

In Vietnam, my children did not understand why I would wear the same shirt, and give away the new shirts to other people. One day, the deacons in our church came to my wife with a new, expensive shirt for me. They kept watching for me to wear the new shirt, but I never wore it.

Soon, they saw a pastor from the countryside wearing the shirt that they gave me. They wondered, "How can this guy from the countryside afford an expensive shirt like this one? It looks like the one we gave to Pastor Ai." They got mad, "I bought this shirt for Pastor Ai because he is General Superintendent, and so he would wear it when he goes out."

I told them, "My mom taught me that when you give someone the best, you will have it forever because they will never forget that you gave them the best. If you give them the old one you do not need anymore, they may not use it, and they will forget it forever."

I became a very wealthy pastor in Vietnam because people understood the principles of giving, and I believed and lived what I taught about tithing and giving. Even in prison, I was a wealthy prisoner. I had more water than other people because people would tithe on their ration of water. When we came to America, many friends tried to tell us how we would have to make money, such as Ruth getting a job.

I told them, "Look, if God is able to take us all the way from Vietnam to America, then He is able to take care of us. He was able to provide our needs in Vietnam, so He is able to provide for our needs in America."

God has been faithful to provide for us to continue to travel in order to preach the Gospel and disciple people all over Southeast Asia and in other parts of the world. Because God has provided for our needs, we are able to continue to bless pastors around the world.

I have also taught these truths to my children. My youngest daughter, Elizabeth, has experienced the fruit of tithing and giving in an unexpected way. When Elizabeth was 16, she was able to get a job working ten hours per week. She made about $62 each week.

The first check she received, she gave 10% to her church, 10% to our ministry, Vietnamese Outreach International, and she was talking with her mom on where she should give another 10%. She was considering giving to one of the missionaries that we knew. Ruth, my wife, said, "Elizabeth, this is your first check." "Yes, that is why I want to give thirty percent," she explained.

"Elizabeth, according to Proverbs, the first check is supposed to be the first fruits offering," Ruth told her. Elizabeth read Proverbs 3:9-10, *Honor the Lord with thy substance, and with the firstfruits of all thine increase: So shall thy barns be filled with plenty, and thy presses shall burst out with new wine.*(KJV)

"Mom, according to the Word of God, I am supposed to give my whole check as the firstfruits to God." I told her, "Honey, do whatever you feel in your heart, but that's the Bible." She said, "Wow, I have to think about it. I was planning on giving only 30%, and now I realize that I must give 100% as the firstfruits offering. I need to pray about this."

Ruth told her, "Honey, you really don't need to pray about this because it's already in the Word of God. He has already told us what we should do."

It took Elizabeth a few days to make this decision because this was the first time in her life that she had a check come to her. She happily made the decision to give her whole check as her firstfruits offering, not because her mom and dad told her to, but because that was what God said to do in His Word.

Less than two months later, she received a notice from Virginia Commonwealth University for a $2000 scholarship. She was faithful to give more than 10% of her income, as do all my children. To us, the tithe (10%) is not giving, it is like paying taxes; it is what we pay back to God. We give more than the tithe to Vietnamese Outreach International and to other missionaries. Because of this, God blesses us abundantly.

Elizabeth remained faithful to pay tithe and to give even on the small income that she had, and she continued to receive various scholarships.

She received one special scholarship to go to school in Doha, Qatar for one semester. It even included a limousine ride from her home to the airport in Washington, DC. After that first semester, she received another scholarship for a second semester, which is very rare.

Because I have believed the promises and applied the principles of giving in my life, I have seen God not only provide for the basics of what He had called me and my wife to do, but He has given us more, besides.

If you do the same thing, you will reap a harvest, and you will be set free from the bondage of poverty. You will be blessed, and God will make you a blessing to others. Give and expect a great harvest!

EPILOGUE

Our vision is for every Vietnamese to hear the Gospel and every believer functioning as a soul winner, cell leader, and church planter to expand the Kingdom of God. Each project described below is a part of the strategy for fulfilling the vision God has given to us.

PROJECTS

Win Souls

Ruth and I continue to go to many nations which employ Vietnamese contract workers. We invite the workers to dinner, and then we share the Good News with them. Then, we lead them to accept Jesus. With your partnership through prayer, intercession and giving, we will surely be able to bring more souls into His kingdom!

Train Soul Winners

After the Vietnamese workers get saved, we train them how to share their testimony and how to present the Good News of Jesus to their beloved one, their families, friends and communities. We need you to partner with us in training and multiplying soul winners for His kingdom!

Equip Cell Leaders

After people are successful in winning souls and starting their cell groups, we need to train them on how to multiply disciples and to become a church planter.

Plant Churches

We then train church planters. Starting off in the sensitive areas that we are working, it is really difficult, but with the power of the Holy Spirit, nothing is impossible. However, we still need you to partner with us in church planting projects to win more souls and start planting more new churches in Laos, Cambodia and Vietnam, particularly in North Vietnam.

Since 1930 the people of North Vietnam have been under communist control and have not had the opportunity to hear the Good News of Jesus Christ. The Vietnamese workers, however, who hear the Good News while they are in other countries are trained and equipped to share the Good News of Jesus Christ when they return to Vietnam.

Will you partner with us to send people back to North Vietnam to share the Good News of Jesus with people who have never heard the Gospel?

Rescue Children

We started Children's Lighthouse Refuge in Cambodia to offer food, clothing, education and discipleship to children at risk of being sold into prostitution or forced labor in order to help with the family finances. Children who have an opportunity for an education and who have food and clothing provided are less likely to be exploited.

The Refuge is meeting these basic needs for the children and also equipping the children to be able to reach out to other children, thereby building up a new generation that not only loves Jesus and lives for Jesus, but who also loves their neighbor. Together, with this young generation, we will turn the "killing fields" into a mission field so that it will become a living field!

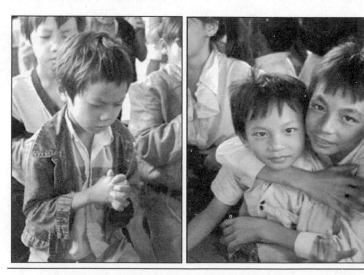

PAUL & RUTH AI – MINISTRIAL SUMMARY

OVERSEAS:

- **REACH**: Reaching Vietnamese Outside of Vietnam (Kuwait, South Korea, Malaysia, Laos, Cambodia) with the Good News of Jesus Christ (Evangelism) and;

- **TEACH**: Disciple them to be Soul Winners, Cell Group Leaders;

- **RELEASE**: Train and prepare them to go back to Vietnam as Church Planters to plant churches all over Vietnam.

CAMBODIA:

- Training Center:

  Every 3 months we have group of Pastors and Church Planters coming from Vietnam, Laos to be trained.

- Light House Children's Refuge Home:

  - *Feeding and teaching Vietnamese & Khmer and the Bible to orphans and children;Providing clothes and necessities to them;*

  - *Train and prepare them to be future Witnesses for Christ and teach them skills for acquiring jobs and better lives.*

VIETNAM:

- Winning Souls
- Planting Churches
- Upgrading Discipleship

LAOS:

We're doing the same method of Reach, Teach & Release.

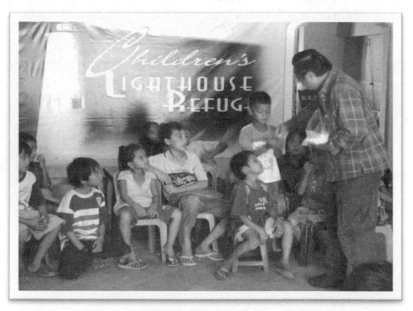

Ps. Paul at the Children's Lighthouse Refuge Home

PARTNERS

"The share of the man who stayed with the supplies is to be the same as that of him who went down to the battle. All will share alike." I Samuel 30:24 (NIV)

If you are interested to know more details of how can you partner with Ruth & I and VOI in these projects to win souls, equip and multiply disciples, plant churches, and rescue children; and to partner with us through prayer, intercession and giving, please feel free to contact us through our contact details as indicated in the next page.

If you are interested in joining one of our mission trips, please feel free to contact us as well.

May God bless you abundantly!

Paul & Ruth Ai

CONTACT INFORMATION

E-mail   : Dr.paulai@gmail.com
           : Dr_paulai@yahoo.com

Website   : www.paulai.com
             www.paulai.net
             www.paulai.org

Facebook   : Paul Ai

Telephone : +1.757.826.1426 Ext.272

Facsimile : +1.757.826.5436

Malaysia : *+60.12.300.1780 [SMS]*

Ps. Paul and Ruth Ai with their five children at their 20 year ministry celebration in 1995

Picture taken at Ps. Paul & Ruth Ai's youngest and only son's wedding at the end of 2014

(Back row-Left to right) Ayham J. & Elizabeth, Esther & husband Daniel Pham with their son Timothy, Ps. Paul Ai, David & wife Jessica, Mrs. Ruth Ai, Baby Ruth & husband Ngoc Phan with their two girls Kyria & Kelcie, Mary & husband Samuel Le with their son Justin. (Front row-Left to right) grandchildren Katherine Phan & Vincent Le

Children and orphans at Children's Lighthouse Refuge in Cambodia

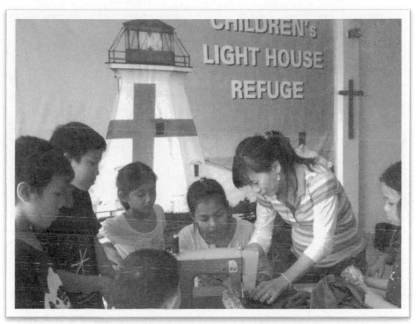

Ps.Ruth teaching the children how to use a sewing machine in Cambodia

Ps. Paul preaching at a New Year Outreach in Cambodia

Feeding children and orphans in Cambodia

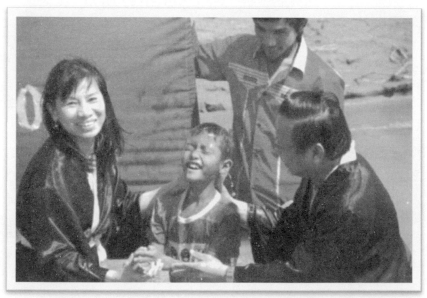
Ps. Paul & Ruth Ai doing water baptism for children and orphans in Cambodia